Nor Shall My Sword Sleep

DAVID BOYLE

First published by Sharpe Books in 2020.

For my mother.

CONTENTS

I, Caractacus – or better still, since Caractacus is a Romanised name – I, Caradoc, am an enforced citizen of Rome and a native of the nations of Britain, as my name should suggest. This is my life and confession to whosoever would like to know the truth of our nations and our lives before we were swallowed up by the so-called civilisation of Rome.

It is an act of vanity, I accept, to write my life in this way, especially for one who, like me, believes that there is a further life to come. But as I know that, since I am the sole, senior representative of my home islands of Britain here in the so-called capital city of the world – who knows our rivers, our misty fields and dark forests – then I believe I have a duty to justify myself.

If I do not explain myself and my actions to my generation and those who come after me, then they may not understand how and why I resisted for so long the tyrannical yoke of Rome – not so much from a horror of their civilisation, but from a pride in our own. I do not trust my Roman neighbours, friendly as they now may seem, to understand our role in Europe as Britons, now and in the future. Nor do I trust the newly Romanised British, my compatriots, to take the pride they should in what sets our islands apart.

I hope my story may encourage them to think afresh.

I - Osen

I had been to Osen before, for my elder brother's election as heir to the high king, near the docks at Osenford. I remember the river rushing past, and the huge hall they say is built at the exact centre of these British islands. But I was jealous of all the attention Togod was receiving and I took little in of the apparently endless rituals as the druids bent over their sacred fires. So I was unprepared for my second visit. I was also now older.

I had been born, as far as I remember, on a blustery night in the sixth winter of the reign of our king, Cunobelin, my father. My mother, who was to become queen, was then one of the warriors of his bodyguard. This fact alone will, I fear, make my Roman readers rise from their couches in alarm, and disbelieve the rest of this account, but I must assure you that we have a different view of the role and relative importance of women and men among us Celtic peoples.

My arrival was unexpected and not entirely welcome as I made my appearance on the rush floor by the open fire in Cunobelin's palace in Camelod. I expect my arrival in the world would have caused more of a stir were it not that, from the same litter, so to speak, my brother Togod had emerged about as long before me as a kettle takes to boil. Those few beats of his heart that made him so little senior to me also made the most enormous difference in our prospects. It meant that he would be the eldest son, legitimised by druid ritual, and he would be prepared to inherit the kingdom by election, as is the way of us Britons.

That was how he came first to Osen and why I came these years later – not to be heir – but to be betrothed to be married, part of my father's obsessive diplomacy around the British isles, designed to sideline Atrebatia and the Belgae and to build alliances against the probability of another Roman incursion.

My first time at Osen, I had felt more than a little resentful of all the attention being lavished on my twin. But I could not forget the huge hall and the roof held up by the trunks of real oak trees, and the gloom around the outside of the room as we watched, while the priest intoned his ceremony by the light of a huge fire in the middle, the smoke disappearing out of a hole in the roof. It was an amazing building, enormous and flat when you were inside it, breath-taking in its size, but conical when you looked at the outside. At that age, I fear I took it for granted.

This time, only a little more mature, I felt thrilled and nervous that I was doing something that only the great men of my father's table – or so I then believed – used to do.

It was the night before the ceremony of my marriage betrothal, when in more ways than one I count my coming of age. It was the day I first met my cousin Cartimandua. It was also a moment of real enlightenment.

This, my second visit, and one of my first journeys outside the borders of my father's kingdom, marked Beltane, so there was if anything more fire to watch hypnotically. I barely noticed the other people present – Fidelma of course, my tutor, my family and household, Cartimandua's family – though my father and the King of Brigantia was absent. I remember, there was a young Roman there, a diplomat determined to be polite to the high king's relatives.

I was by then sixteen or perhaps a few more winters old and I was the centre of attention perhaps for the first time in my life. I found I hardly enjoyed it as much as I expected. People fussed around me.

"You need a brooch to hold that cloak together, and not that one," said Fidelma. My mother glared at me to show she had overheard.

"And you need a comb through that mat of straw hair too," said Togod, teasing.

"I think you look lovely," said my younger sister Imogen, who always took pity on me whether it was necessary or not.

If being the centre of attention warranted all this concentration on my appearance, then I could do without it, I thought. Still, what could I do? I made a mental note to make myself as scarce as possible until just before the ritual the following afternoon.

"Thank you, lovely Imo," I said. I knew that, for Imogen, I was the most precious person in the whole world. Sometimes this knowledge hung heavily.

I was not the heir, and yet I remained a younger prince, so I was in a peculiar position, both of the royal house and forged into the great spider's web of diplomacy that my father had woven as high king, and yet free to come and go – barely granted my father's attention except when he was angry with either of us. Both trained to be a warrior but also free to become a druid and lawyer in my learning as well. This was how I first came to be in Rome, as I shall tell.

If I had not loved and revered by brother Togod, I might perhaps have resented my spare existence, but I did. "I would not swap my life for yours for all the gold in the Roman treasury," I told him once, after he had boasted about a hunting exploit of his.

"Unusually, you are right, Caradoc," he said. "I lead the life of a dog. I feed well and sometimes I'm let out for a run, but the rest of the time I am tied by a leash to my master."

We laughed and for a time, I knew him as *doggie* (Latin: *'canis parvum'*). Most of the time, we played and talked as if we shared one mind, just as we were almost made from one body – though he was dark and I was fair. There came a time when this was perhaps to save my life. Otherwise, there was no victory in battle – mainly the occasional tussle with the Atrebates by the Thames – no achievement in the hunting field, no hart or boar slain by either of us that the other did not revel in. My main memory of my childhood years was his smiling face. Above all, we agreed as the years went by about the one political issue that divided everyone: what our attitude should be to the Romans.

Surrounding the temple buildings at Osen, along the bank of the river, were a number of small tents and booths for visitors, and – because this ceremony was for me – I had been given a booth of my own to prepare myself mentally, I believe. Fidelma came in and out, overflowing with advice and instructions – she had once been a druidic priest there – so the moment I was to be alone, and one of the first moments in my life I had ever been so, did not come until I turned in for the night, with a glimpse of the stars clear above me through the window and the sounds of the water running fast through the shallows.

It was a homely, comforting sound, and I lay there listening and feeling a little nervous about what would be expected of me the following day. Yet something seemed out of place. Was it scratching or breathing? Was it in fact coming from just below the window?

I got quietly to my feet, fetched my hunting knife from under my bedding and peered out. There was nothing there.

It felt strange. I was unused to sleeping on my own. Was this some kind of trick by Togod? That certainly seemed the most likely explanation. I slipped back into the shadows.

Then, suddenly, I was grabbed from behind by what seemed at first like a huge snake, but then was clearly a human being of about my height. I swung round and could hardly believe what I saw. A girl, some years older than myself judging by her lines and curves, with dark hair and darker eyes, held me worryingly close.

"So," she said haughtily. "This is the boy my father has chosen for me as a husband. And – wait…"

She put her fingers to her lips, walking slowly around me in my night garb, which was little or nothing. She made what I hoped was an approving sound.

"Yes, he's young and a little scrawny. But he has nice shoulders, good thighs and buttocks, and…"

I confess the attention was exciting me.

"Yes, well, my name is Cartimandua, and I have come to check over my investment. To make doubly sure I am ready for tomorrow."

"Check over? Your investment?"

I had heard rumours about Cartimandua. I had obviously

questioned anybody likely to be able to tell me anything about her once I had heard we were to be betrothed. Fidelma was noticeably tight-lipped, but others had told me she was beautiful and determined. She was clearly both. They also implied she enjoyed some sexual power, and in this they were also absolutely correct.

"You see, my dear Caradoc, I wanted to test you out – and now I'm going to. So kiss me."

As I have told my Roman hosts many times, British women are not as meek as Roman women. They know what they want, as men do and – if they can take their pleasure, well, they take it. But even so, I was taken aback by a seduction by one so close to my own age. I was no virgin, but equally I had imagined royal women to be a little more reserved. Or at least to pretend to be.

"So you are shy then? Come on, this is your great chance too. Let us know each other as we should not before the ceremony tomorrow – as would upset our ancestors if they knew!"

So I kissed her full on the lips, and then some other places as well, during the night that followed. And when we had discovered everything we could about each other's bodies, we turned to our minds. Only once were we nearly discovered, when Fidelma put her head through my door, and we dived beneath the eiderdown, while I made the kind of sounds that implied I was asleep, while Cartimandua giggled beneath me. We talked until the light began to seep into the sky. Not long afterwards, I awoke from a snooze and found she had stolen away.

But this was not before we had exchanged opinions on everything from the way we would behave in the morning to persuade our elders we were meeting for the first time, to the right occupation for the twin but younger brother of a king.

Of course, even at that age, I still longed to be a warrior, rather than an occasional protected observer of small battles, but I had been studying under Fidelma for fourteen years now. So why did I have a female druid as my tutor, she asked?

"And why should I not?" I felt defensive.

5

"Oh come on! Does your brother have a female tutor? Have you never asked?"

Of course I had asked.

"It is said to be a way to keep the world in balance," I said, perhaps a little unconvinced. "Togod has a male tutor, so I must have a female one. Or so I have been told."

"As if you were a married couple!" she guffawed.

"As though I were a man," I replied. I said it with more bitterness than I actually felt. I knew and accepted the process whereby, as a twin brother, I must in some way be a wife to Togod. Symbolically, of course, and only until we were grown. Yet now we were grown and more than of age, I still longed for it, despite my druidic studies among the Silurians.

We ventured onto the mischievous topic of the future of the Atrebates, even then struggling in the net woven for them by my father. And the tortured political question of relations with Rome. Would we face a nation in battle, as our Gaulish cousins had over the previous century, though this battle seemed pretty endless for the Gauls? In short, this was a question of tactics: should we let them come, as it seemed inevitable that they would – if only for our tin reserves – or should we resist?

It goes without saying that Togod and I followed my father's campaigns that brought pressure on Atrebatia and their Belgic allies in the south, and the assimilation of the Trinovantes around the city of Trinovan, with cheers and enthusiasm. We believed in him, as people did in those days, and especially after the alliance he negotiated with King Esuprast, the King of Icenia. We bemoaned his diplomatic setbacks and assisted in the rituals of giving thanks after his military breakthroughs. We also followed his lead on the great question of our age – our relationship with the Romans and what shape it ought to take.

There were broadly three opinions and they were constantly expressed. There were the *realists* who believed that, sooner or later, some Caesar would come knocking with his legions and it made sense to come to some kind of accommodation. There were the *enthusiasts* who positively welcomed the prospect of being subsumed into the Roman empire – mainly to protect us against the warlike barbaric German tribes who occasionally arrived on our shores.

But as the sons of Cunobelin, my brother and I were the archetypal *resisters*. We wanted to be ready for the moment when the eagles landed, to knit together some kind of common defence to protect the civilisation we loved.

I can hardly pretend that every ploughboy and farmer's daughter had a view about these matters – though I sometimes wondered. But in the circles I moved in, among the warriors and druids around Camelod, this was the live issue of the age. There were times when we believed that the successors of Julius Caesar were about to return, and then the arguments became more heated as we began to work out how we could generate the kind of mighty response mobilised so successfully by my great ancestor Cassivelaun, that we might prevent Tiberius or his legions sneaking back across the ocean that divides us from the world.

It was my secret dream of those years that I would be called upon to defend our island against Caesar's legions and would somehow succeed magnificently. I believed the dream was shared by Togod, though perhaps in retrospect he grew more responsible before I did. Be careful what you dream of, my druid tutor Fidelma used to say – and in this respect she was absolutely right. I have few regrets about my life, so what could I have done differently? But even so, I wish I could have seen the future a little more clearly than I did.

Perhaps I was deluded because of who I was, because nobody ever expressed in my hearing, during my childhood and youth, any opinion that my father's policy might be mistaken. Of course I knew such opinions were held – how could I not with a tutor as worldly as Fidelma? But she always explained the flaws in their argument and I assumed they were widely understood.

I need hardly say I believed then, and now in fact, passionately in resisting Rome. Everyone I had ever met said the same: perhaps they did not truly believe it – indeed it is hard to interpret the last few winters in any other way. But

Cartimandua was the first person who admitted any kind of ambiguity on the issue.

She did more than simply confess it – as if anyone could drag any kind of confession out of Cartimandua against her will. She argued the case for Rome with an unexpected passion. She knew the arguments in both directions, but she knew what she wanted.

"Don't you want warm feet at home, Caradoc? You know they have heating under their floors…"

I was incredulous. "Are you seriously saying you want to turn your back on everything we love – just to warm your toes?"

"Of course not. Why should we have to choose? We just need some kind of arrangement. Don't you think we would benefit from that kind of city living – so cosmopolitan, so luxurious, so exciting? Why do we want to rule over our little corners of the frozen north when we could live in such style? Instead of woad and mumbo-jumbo from the druids? They're not so different from us, the Romans, except that they're richer…"

"How could we be ourselves and be slaves of the Romans," I said. "The two things contradict each other."

I said it quickly but I was disturbed. I had never met anyone before who wanted any kind of *rapprochement* with the Romans. I realised I had, in this respect at least, led a sheltered life.

"Oh, you men! All you think about is fighting and glory, or the stars if you are one the druids. Haven't you ever wanted to wander through a great city, or to hear the crowds roar in the Circus Maximus in Rome. Or lie for the night on furs from the Black Sea?"

"Well, it isn't all *I* think about," I said, changing the subject with another erotic embrace.

**

After Cartimandua had crept out of my hut, I stood for a while outside, feeling the night air on my naked chest. I was about to receive my second shock in the dark.

The first I knew of my attacker was a flash of polished iron from some kind of weapon. A moment later, the blade was against my throat and I was pinned from behind by a tall man who – judging by his hairless arm – could have been little older than I was myself.

I was too surprised to be frightened to start with, though, as I realised the fellow's strength, the fear began to rise. I had to act quickly.

I felt for a second his grip on my left arm slacken and I slipped it free and drove my elbow into his guts. He doubled up and I was able to swing round and grab his sword hand. I slammed it back against the door frame. The blade clattered onto the flagstones.

He was now between myself and the door to safety and I could see him before he swung at me. I kicked the sword away and found myself gasping as I did so: I looked into his face to try and work out who my attacker was, only to find that there was nothing there. The man appeared to have no face. Just black.

A moment or so later, I understood this was no demon from the forest, come to punish me for what I had been doing; he was wearing a mask. I could see him glancing round looking for his weapon, and realised that – although a black mask was initially terrifying, it now getting in his way.

I tried to hit him and he parried me and I doubled up myself, winded.

"Who … are … you?" I asked, puffing like a dog in the heat. "Why hide behind a mask if you want to kill me?"

This time, I recovered enough to get a blow in. He wiped a small rivulet of blood from his lips. I was unsure which of us it had come from.

"Because…," he said, also panting. "Because I have sworn an oath to the King of Brigantia." That was clear enough. Now I had heard his voice and his dialect, I could confirm that he spoke the truth about where he hailed from.

We struggled some more. Then, simultaneously, we both saw his sword on the ground under the bushes and leaped for it. He got there first – he was taller than me – but I kicked him hard behind his shins as he reached down. And he fell across it.

There then followed what seemed to me for many years afterwards the fight for my life, as we rolled around in the dust exchanging blows. Then there was the sword – it was in my hand. Now, wouldn't I have to kill him if I was to save myself – unless…

There was the river running by. I certainly didn't want to kill him – for one thing, he would have been the first person I had ever killed. So I flung it as hard as I could towards the river bank. We both heard a small splash.

"Now," I said. "You know, all I have to do is shout and people will come running."

He sat there on the ground, clearly furious with himself as well as me.

"Yeah, but your too fucking proud to do it," he said.

I knew he was right.

"So tell me, stranger. What oath did you make to the King of Bragantia?"

"I swore to protect his daughter."

"I also would like to protect her," I said, a little naively perhaps.

My attacker spat on the round.

"That's right. To protect her from poncie southerners like you."

I confess, I was beginning to find the encounter funny, but I dared not laugh.

"I don't understand. First, she came here of her own free will and, second, tomorrow we will be betrothed to be married…"

This enraged him. "Listen, you stuck up wanker. You want me to kill you with bare hands? What you're saying this betrothal has happened already? What, you couldn't resist a few sweetmeats a bit early, eh? Now piss off to the devil, will you. And after tomorrow, you go touching any princesses again, and you'll find yourself with more than me and my friends to contend with."

He was gone almost as suddenly as he had arrived. I thought

10

of him often during the day, wondering really whether he had friends at all on what must be a lonely and obsessive quest to keep Cartimandua in a state of purity.

The following day – as I waited for the interminable ritual to be finally over – I thought also of those hours I had spent with Cartimandua, and in intimate connection we had forged in what may have been the most enlightening night of my life up to that point. There seemed to be no limit to what I had learned under the stars, with the sound of the endless river rippling into the distance – from my first erotic encounter with an equal, right through to a better understanding about what we felt, we Britons, about the prospects of a Roman intervention in our lives.

When I woke at dawn, it was to be pampered and dressed for our ceremony, explaining away the cuts and bruises on my face – I forget how. It was an exhausting and terrifying prospect.

**

"By the old gods, by old Brigit's beard, these druids move so slowly," I heard my uncle exclaim by noon, before we had even begun. "Whole empires can rise and fall between their rituals."

I thought it probable that he would not last the whole ceremony.

Sure enough, after a wait of what seemed just moments, he had forced his way out to the cold edges of the ritual, far from the growing blaze, then out through the crowds of druids in training and the labouring families and villagers who gathered for these occasions and was away, followed shortly afterwards by Cartimandua's uncle. It occurred to me that the attention paid to our betrothal had reduced somewhat since our respective fathers had set our course to seal their mutual agreement. But we were neither of us the heirs – it was hard to swallow, but there it was.

A silence fell after they had left, which was filled by the arrival of the chief druid, Bran, in his long white robes,

followed by group of lesser druids. I kept looking over at
Cartimandua, but she was studiously ignoring me. Perhaps,
like me, she was irritated at getting so little attention. My
father had been there for Togod's ceremony. I knew that
perfectly well.

Afternoon winter darkness was now falling outside the hall,
through the narrow windows, and our faces were lit by the
central fire, now burning brightly and warmly enough to force
us further into the shadows. I saw Fidelma send me a look of
encouragement, together with a hint of something else. Was it
fear? Surely not. Something unnerving seemed to be going on
which I did not understand.

The druids were now intoning their ritual. The heat was
exhausting and I still had no real understanding what was
happening. It was only when the druids threw pails of water
onto the burning charcoal, turning them black in big hissing
clouds of steam, that I began to get some inkling of what was
going to be expected of me. This was to be not just a betrothal;
it was also a belated coming of age ritual – which would take
the form of some kind of ordeal.

Fidelma was next to me by then. She whispered in my year.
"Caradoc, do not fear – that is my strong advice to you.
Remember what I have shown you over the years and you will
be fine. There will be no pain. Just remember that – *there will
be no pain…*"

I only had to walk three or four paces. I knew I must do so
slowly and deliberately and that I knew how to leave my body
during those moments. I had learned that much as a druid. I
also knew that Cartimandua was watching, along with nearly
everyone else. Togod gripped my arm to strengthen me. My
lovely sister Imogen hugged me around the waist, and then I
was led off behind the screen to be ritually washed by an
ancient priest who flicked my naked body with a few drops of
holy water. And then made me drink a warm concoction so
disgusting that I hardly noticed that everyone seemed different
by the time I had drained the cup.

That was an ordeal, I said to myself, chuckling a little. And
by the time I had finished enjoying my own joke, I was there -

dreamily about to step onto the hot coals.

I no longer cared, thanks to whatever herbal magic I had been administered. All I knew was that I had to get to the other side without embarrassing myself. I lifted my leg and put my foot on the hot ledge. There was no pain, I told myself.

The next thing I knew I was stepping off the other side, and a great cheer went up. I was just in time to catch sight of Cartimandua cheering along with everyone else, and then I collapsed.

When I awoke, I heard subdued murmuring. I looked up, and could see Imogen talking to the Roman diplomat, and putting some meat to her lips. I was covered in a great oxhide. Fidelma was stroking my feet.

"You did well, my son," she said.

"Fidelma, who is that Roman talking to Imogen?" I suddenly distrusted his hungry look.

"The younger one? I believe he is from the Scapula family. His father is a general and a relation of the imperial family. But how are you?"

I realised there was a dull ache coming from my feet. Then there was suddenly a hush.

"What's happening?" I asked.

"The priest is coming around. He's slept this past hour - nearly as long as you have."

I wanted to ask more about Scapula. Nor did I know what Bran was supposed to say, but it was soon clear that something had not gone according to plan. The first I realised of this was when the chief druid clutched his head as he came round from his holy trance. I watched fascinated as the other druidic priests dashed to his side and watched the intense whisperings that followed. Clearly he had not, as intended, dreamed what he expected to dream.

I wonder now why it is that our priests insist on this kind of divinatory ritual at moments like these. They seem such a hostage to fortune. But at the time, I found their discomfort amusing. This time, I did catch Cartimandua's eye and we grinned conspiratorially.

Bran came out from behind the translucent curtains that hid

us both and stared, a little crazily, at the crowd. I see now that he was searching for my father to make sure the high king did not witness this particular prophecy.

"What's he going to say?" I whispered to Fidelma, suddenly nervous.

"You know, the truth about the world…"

The tradition was, I believe, that the dreaming priest will say his or her stuff immediately on waking, in perfect rhyming couplets. So few people survive who remember such things, now that so few druids remain. This is not what happened here.

Finally, his assistant made the announcement:

"They will be happy,
and the future knows each name.
Both will rule their nations
And they will not be the same…"

What did it mean? That I would rule a nation – not the same one as she would? As the words exploded around me, I had a moment to think about this authoritative prophecy. I looked for Cartimandua, but she was gone. Was that what it meant?

Furious officials were remonstrating with Bran: and I realised that neither Cartimandua or myself were actually the cause. What had been predicted was a great upset, which was why the Brigantian delegation had stormed out and clearly my own was preparing to do the same. I could see by the defensive raised shoulders and open arms of Bran that he was saying something like – "what could I do?" I glanced at Togod and he was laughing. He had hardly taken this prophecy as the insult of the kind it was said to have been.

It was as if neither of the great kings, who should have been present – and perhaps Bran would have suppressed his dream if they had been - would succeed in their plans for succession, and perhaps failed to understand what they were doing when they betrothed their children to each other.

**

14

I remember little about the day and night of that visit to Osen, and barely thought about my coming of age – except of course for my peculiar night with Cartimandua and then her protector. But I have a faint memory of the feasting that took place that evening and the smell of roasting boar which suffused the whole occasion, and sitting on the rushes on the ground, next to Togod and my father, after he had finally arrived to seal whatever murky deal he had planned with the Brigantians, allowed to taste for the first time the great mead cup as it perambulated around us.

That, and listening to Bran's interminable songs as the evening turned to night, and the great room seemed to sway around me.

Very early the next morning, before we had been able to recover from the wine, I went with the others from Camelod to the dockside at Osenford to take the ship up the Thames river and home. It was too dark to set sail, so Togod and I lay wrapped in our travelling cloaks on the deck by the brazier. Nobody spoke of the prophecy again, but of course I thought of it in weak moments, however hard I had tried to put it out of my head.

Fidelma told me later that my father had summoned his closest advisors and decided that I should continue my studies, which meant druid school in Caer Leon to learn about astronomy. I was interested in the paths of the stars – who could not be in Britain where it is dark for so long – but I was sorry that, by deciding that I should deepen by knowledge of druid wisdom, my father appeared to be sidelining me away from the diplomatic work which he had been expecting me to master before.

Because, although he preened himself like a warrior, and I feel sure would like to be remembered as one, my father was at heart a strategist, a diplomat. He was prepared to fight – and his reign certainly saw him fight the Trinovantes and the Atrebates – but he tried to achieve his objectives without fighting. It was diplomacy above all that he used to sideline the threat from Atrebatia pushing up from the south bank of the Thames when I had been younger, its traditional boundary with us.

But it was Togod who accompanied my father on his endless rounds, his long diplomatic journeys. Nobody was so much in the saddle as he, on those long winding journeys on the old trade roads, along the downs or through the marshes from forest to forest, from royal court to royal court, sidelining, connecting, stoking up awareness of the greater threat – from Rome.

I know from my studies in Osenford after Caer Leon that this threat was often dismissed by some of the younger princelings who, like Cartimandua, believed it was old-fashioned. Rome was fashionable in those days and so were Romans, for their cities, their luxury, their sheer technological brilliance – why should we remain a backwater in the civilised world? That was what I was told wherever I went in those days. Why could we not aspire to being part of an imperial power greater than ourselves? Anything to hold back the German raiders we kept hearing about, but never actually saw.

It was only later that my father began to include me in his efforts, and I feel glad that he did so, and that I began to know the great Cunobelin a little before he died. I have had reason since to thank the Lord that I sat and learned at his feet.

But that was shortly before I had been for one short and, it seems now, tragic visit to Rome itself. What I saw there turned me from a fascinated sceptic to a passionate advocate of British defence.

II - Rome

I have mentioned Imogen only in passing. I felt close to Togod of course – we had shared a womb together after all – but I loved my sister with a great and overwhelming sense of her goodness that, since she was stolen from us, has only grown in intensity. She was close to us in age as well, which divided me more from my studious youngest sister, Gwladys.

That may have been why my father chose me to escort Imogen to her marriage which he had arranged with the son of an up-and-coming Roman commander and administrator, a distant relative of the imperial family no less, a man I would have occasion to know a little myself later. Of his son I knew nothing. Nor I believe did my father, though I gather he had been advised over this alliance by one of the Roman officials who used to hang around our court at Camelod. Like the Roman diplomat I had glimpsed – though he may have invited himself – to my betrothal ceremony in Osen.

It happened that my tutor, Fidelma, was urging me to study history, once I had completed my astrological studies at Caer Leon. She had been keen for me to have a spell of study in Rome at the famous library at Porticus Octaviae. The two objectives were soon melded into one and, feeling serious and with two bodyguards and a golden dagger as a wedding present, Imogen and I set off for the beaches along the river near Trinovan to take a ship for Gaul. I remember the coloured ships and sails dragged up the strand downstream from the great bridge there. I had seen them before, from across the known world, but this was the first time I had embarked in one.

As the wind filled the sail in the port of Trinovan, Imogen turned to me with tears rolling down her cheeks. "Oh, Caradoc," she said. "I don't know if I can live without you and Togod and Fidelma." I should explain that our mother had died some winters before.

God forgive me: I did not take her seriously and tried to jolly her along.

"Imogen, I understand. But I will be there to help you settle in and make friends. I can think of women who would love beyond all things to live in Rome amidst all that luxury, with the skins from Russia or the olive oil from Palestine, with underfloor heating, warm baths and sunshine. And the fashion! You will be the most fashionable woman in Europe..!"

Cartimandua crossed my mind. It had been some winters also since my strange night with her, but I thought of it most days even then.

"I feel like I am being disposed of by our father as if I was one of his chess pieces."

I rather agreed, I was twenty-four winters old by then and yet my father's relationship with Brigantia had cooled, which meant that my marriage remained unresolved. We were both chess pieces, but at least I could remain at home with my family.

How many times since have I thought of that conversation with shame and wished I had acted differently. All I can say is that I was carrying out my father's wishes.

**

I could not say I warmed to Julius Ostorius Scapula, when I first met him. I rose when he came in the room, out of Celtic politeness, along with our two bodyguards, Gwalchmai and Verkingor, and I laid my sword before my host, as a future brother-in-law should do. I immediately recognised him too, as the Roman witness to my ordeal and betrothal at Osen. He must have seen Imogen there and requested her.

You will ask, I know, what my impressions of Rome were that first visit. The truth was I had experienced nothing like it before. This huge city, for someone from a nation where – except for places like Trinovan or Camelod - we have shunned city living, seemed to both of us both monstrous and extraordinary at the same time.

The buildings were lovely but also less impressive that our best buildings. Even so, the beauty of the towers reaching up above the forum was staggering and sublime, the poverty and the cruelty was not. I had not yet seen their gladiators in action at that stage, nor seen the baying crowd at the games calling for blood, as I did later in my visit, but I saw the sheer waste - a whole side of beef, a prize cut, thrown into the Tiber to show the wealth of the man who threw it.

Or who had it thrown. This was, after all, a city of slaves stolen from across the empire.

I had been trained in the druid way for many winters – most of my life – and have since understood something of the way of Christ, and both cried out in the face of a city built on those abuses.

It was clear, though, since we arrived in Rome, exhausted from our voyage from Massalia that something else was in the air. There was the dust from the direction of the forum and the most heartfelt cheers, and something that animated people. It was subtle but obvious.

"What is happening? *Quod suus fieri*?" I said, aware that this was the first sentence in the Latin taught me by Fidelma which I had spoken in the home city of the language.

"Where've you been!" said the man I asked, across his shop counter. It wasn't a question. "It's the new emperor, Gaius – Caligula, we call him."

Why would they call an emperor by the size of his boots?

"What! Tiberius is dead?"

The man held out his arms as if only the most stupid person in the whole world could ask such a question.

My father had come a little clearer to me before we set out for Trinovan. "Caradoc, my boy," he had said. "You duties on this trip are clear. First and foremost, to keep Imogen safe. Second, to get to know her new family and to see if you can find out Tiberius' intentions: I believe he has set his face against an invasion of Britain for the time being - but I don't know for certain. It will be hard to meet the emperor, who is I know a recluse, but third - if you meet his close advisers - impress on them our will to resist. Fourth, report your impressions to me. In the meantime, I know you also have your studies. Do you understand?"

"Yes, father," I said, grateful at what I considered to be my advanced age to finally be given a task by him, I was determined to fulfil his instructions to the absolute letter.

So, now, if Tiberius was gone, then his successor – this Gaius – might vary his priorities and I clearly had to keep my ears open. Presumably, nobody would yet know, perhaps not even Gaius, what his attitude to Britain was likely to be. It seemed to me, naive as I was, that he was no military man like his two predecessors – and I was comforted by that fact.

As it was, all I really had to go on was the delighted reaction of the crowd to his accession, which seemed to me to be encouraging. Imogen and I stared at his procession as it passed us by some days later – the soldiers and the children singing anthems. Everyone seemed delighted to be shot of Tiberius. What was unnerving was the news that 160,000 prisoners were to be put to death in celebration.

**

My first impressions of my future brother-in-law were not encouraging either as I laid my sword before him.

"So, you bring me my barbarian bride," he said as I presented myself at his father's home, while Imogen waited upstairs.

For a moment, I did not know what to say. Neither, it seemed, did his other guests. I decided to pretend, or perhaps to assume, that this pompous remark had been intended as a joke. So I laughed and the other guests - there always appeared to be guests at the Scapula mansion - laughed uproariously. Still, it irritated me that he appeared to have made a joke at the expense of my sister and I could see in his eyes that he thought he had the better of me in the encounter.

I shook my head at Verkingor at my side, to say that we would not yet be taking offense. Next time, I said to myself - next time he tells a joke like that one, our friend will not be receiving his golden dagger. And where he least expects.

"I am anxious to meet her, joking apart," said Scapula.

"We barbarians choose our moments well," I said,

deliberately enigmatically. "I will bring my sister tomorrow morning, if that is acceptable."

"No, I am meeting the new consul in the morning. You may come in the afternoon…"

I was, I confess, taken aback by this tone and wondered whether I had inadvertently insulted the man. It was another early sign which I hopelessly failed to recognise. Nor did I understand a broad hint from one of the women there.

"I know your island a little," she said to me. "I have been to Trinovan. Tell me, do you like Rome?"

I hardly knew what to say. "It is extraordinary," I said, "and terrifying too."

She nodded with understanding.

"It isn't always quite what it seems here," she said. "You know, you should keep an eye out for your sister after the wedding. Scapula is young but his beard is a little - er, blue."

"Thank you for the advice. I intend to."

I stared at my new brother-in-law wondering what the phrase referred to. He had no beard and the stubble I could see emerging on his chin at the end of the day seemed more red than blue.

It was all a little strange.

Yet Imogen liked him when they met the following and my fears - such as they were - began to subside. And as we waited for the wedding, Imogen and I, when I was not engaged on my father's business, talking to as many diplomats and officials as I could manage to, we walked together down the streets of Rome from the Palatine to the Appian Way. I grew to love my sister especially now that we had been thrown with time to spare into each other's company. She was also reassuring me.

"Of course I am sad to leave you all, but I can work for you in Rome. I can listen and I can write to you. And I always knew I would have to go one day – it is the lot of royal women, as we both know."

"You are right," I said. "I too have been thinking of such things. We Celts, we British, are more enlightened about women, I believe. They can do as much as they wish as men can. And yet we have these areas - these spots - of blindness, do we not? Either way, Imogen, I will return, every few years, if I can to see you. And we will write to each other too, can we not?"

At the same time, the other side of Rome, the uncivilised side, was also becoming most horribly clear to me. Nor was it just the filthy streets and the beggars, beyond anything I had ever seen, even in Trinovan. Julius' father, the general, introduced me to an obese senator who invited me to his box at the Circus Maximus. "You will like the next item on the programme," he said, with a lascivious giggle.

I had heard about the circus before - who has not? - and knew and now witnessed for myself the pointless sacrifice of brave gladiators, captured soldiers from all over the known world – and possibly beyond it. But nothing prepared me for the scene of degradation that followed, as men and women were forced to have sex with wild animals. With few exceptions, most of them were savaged and gored or eaten bloodily before anything could be managed, but the senator was sweating and on the edge of his seat. In the audience, I saw whole families - men, women and children watching it all with rapt excitement. "If this is civilisation…," I began to say to my host, before remembering the purpose of my journey and ending the sentence with a more diplomatic silence.

I thanked the one God whom we druids served that Imogen had not been with me on that occasion. She is so often moved by the plight of others and some of the scenes I witnessed would have haunted her. But I realised then what I know now - that, if we were to save our corner of Europe from this kind of civilisation, so that our gentle but loving ways might survive for future generations - so that people would never *own* each other by virtue of their wealth - then we would in the end have to fight.

I had the first inkling of what became a growing conviction: that my own country and the nations within it had a role – not as the saviour of Europe perhaps - but as a guarantor that someone might, one day, live as God might want us to – and to begin therefore to stitch heaven and earth back together again. That generation by generation, perhaps, we would bear the responsibility to face down tyrannies, of intense kinds unimagined in my own lifetime.

This I still believe, but could not prove.

This might seem at first the somewhat immodest or vainglorious rantings of a madman. Nor can I claim that I thought these things through at the Circus Maximus, yet it was during that visit, watching a poor mother fighting to protect her infant from the jaws of a hungry striped beast, that I first understood the threat to the world that Rome represented.

Afterwards, I began to fear for my beloved Imogen in that city and hastened to see her, as she prepared for her wedding the following day. But she was with her future father-in-law and they were laughing, and my fears subsided again for a while.

"Caradoc!" she shouted happily. "Join us, please! My husband's father – Publius Ostorius Scapula – was telling me the gossip in Rome. He says that Gaius is considered quite mad. Can you believe that? It is said that he wants to make one of his horses a consul!"

I looked from one to the other and thought I saw genuine enjoyment on both their faces. I felt happier as a result. I even began to set aside Julius' offhand manner. Perhaps it was nerves, after all, not arrogance.

**

The wedding day dawned warm and beautiful and soon I was watching in amazement as the various rituals were set out. I had not been asked to be one of the ten formal witnesses, so I had time on my hands – and I could enjoy the cutting of the bread with a sword and the lighting of the torch, watching three high priests trying to outdo each other in the volume of their voices. And then to hear the noise and smell of the pig and its blood when it had its throat slit.

It was during the banquet that followed that I received my second great shock. I still do not know who the speaker was, though I know his name. Valarius wore multiple armbands in bronze and other metals and he had drunk deeply from the

Scapula's household generosity. He was also ribbing and poking at a man I knew to be the guest of honour, and was probing him drunkenly about the new emperor and his new foreign policy.

The honoured guest was careful what he was saying, aware perhaps that the bride at this wedding was a princess of a foreign nation. I saw him check who was in the room before he gave his clipped answers, seeing me and watching me to see if I was listening. I pretended not to but, in truth, it was hard to avoid hearing what was said.

"Come on, you're among friends here," said Valarian, slurring his words. "Tell us! How - I mean WHAT does our emperor plan for Germany and Gaul and Britain?"

"It is too early to say, I fear. I can say nothing."

Valarian burped loudly.

"Come on, there's no need to be standoffish, just because you are such pals with the Emperor. You know as well as I do what the plans are. I simply ask: when do we go?"

The honoured guest was now looking deeply nervous and glancing round, aware that there were other British guests somewhere in the room. But Valarian had not finished. Now he leapt up and danced in the middle of the room.

"Yes! Yes! We go to Britain now," he shouted, in some ecstacy. "And I shall own all the tin mines in the world and I'll be as rich as Croesus. So tell me I'm wrong - if you dare…"

The honoured guest now leapt up in his seat.

"You have partaken too much of this wedding. Someone, take him outside and introduce him to a horse trough or a water butt. Preferably upside down!"

He was hustled outside by the servants and slaves and I pretended to continue my pointless conversation about the differences between Gaulish and British women. But of course, I was completely alert. This was precisely the kind of intelligence that my father had asked me to listen out for. It was not definitive, but it seemed very much as if this new emperor Gaius – who everyone seemed to call 'Little Boots', for reasons I did not then understand – was indeed planning some kind of raid or full-scale invasion of my homeland.

**

For the rest of the evening, I began to plan how I might confirm it one way or another. The following day, I went to meet the British druid living in Rome, who my host the general had managed to find to take part in the ceremony.

I walked past the Forum, and finally found Divisiac where I had been told he would be, at the Library.

"Please get up, man!" I said, as he recognised me and fell to his knees. "I am merely a trainee druid myself, studying here at the Porticus Octaviae. I am grateful to see the pale skin of a Briton. What brought you to Rome?"

"I came with the druids under Augustus. My task is, slowly but permanently, to establish a druidic college here in the city, though I may not be able to if present trends continue."

"You mean the uncivilising of Rome? I too have been to the Circus Maximus."

"Then you will know the kind of horror I refer to. May I talk openly, my lord?"

I urged him to do so.

"I had heard of your arrival here only a few days ago. We Britons keep our ears to the ground about the arrivals and departures of our fellow country people. But your sister - I did not understand was who she was. If I had done, I would have begged you to reconsider the marriage."

A cold shiver went down my spine. It was as if he had spoken fears which I had barely even articulated to myself.

"Please go on."

"The general is an honourable man, though a weak one. But his son, your brother-in-law Julius, is not. He has a reputation as a violent, er … bigoted…"

Stop, stop…

There is saying in my country that a cold hand clutched my heart. If ever a cold hand clutched mine, it was at that moment.

"Are you sure? You are absolutely certain?"

"I fear so, my lord. This is his third wedding and the last two died in peculiar circumstances, it is said by his hand." Divisiac

25

stopped solemnly and there was silence.

I was thinking as quickly as I could, waves of fear and guilt passed through me. How could I have delivered my most precious person in the world into the arms of a monster? Could I have dared to ask my father to reconsider his decision – just because I personally wanted to visit Rome and was flattered that he had entrusted me with the task of delivery? What would he say if I brought her home again?

"Then, please, advise me," I said. "How can I best get her back and take her to safety?"

"It isn't easy. You must understand that marriage in Rome isn't the equal partnership it has always been in Britain, at least since civilisation reached our shores. Once a Roman marries a woman, he owns her – just like they own houses or oxen or slaves. They are his property. If you were just to steal her away, you would be accused of theft."

"You mean not much has changed since they carried off the Sabine women?"

I paced around the room. "Then I need a reason. Cruelty? Or misbehaviour? Or perhaps my father could need her home?"

Divisiac looked sceptical. "The last line would be difficult to prove since you have only just taken the trouble to bring her out here. Let me think..."

"No, I must go to her – will you come with me? I don't want to put you in an impossible position."

"No, I shall come," he said, bravely. "Let me get my books."

We hurried through the Forum towards the river, but – before we reached its banks – the streets seemed suddenly blocked. It was strange that they seemed so unfamiliar and I remembered no edifice there before that blocked our way. Divisiac told me later that it was a relatively common experience in Rome, a city where buildings can spring up virtually overnight.

It added to my sudden shift in mood and dislocation.

We reached my sister's new home and I asked to see her. To my intense relief, she bounded into the room looking intensely happy, and my determination softened.

I took her for a walk, ostensibly to see the new building that seemed to have sprung up almost overnight. But she shook her head vigorously at the idea that her husband was anything other than a paragon of virtue and charity, a kind man, she said: "Yes, he has a short temper, but then doesn't our father? I'm used to moods and moody men. And he has pleased me," she said shyly. "I shall grow to love him. I believe and pray I will."

"Yes, but nobody in their right mind would encourage you to marry a man like our father," I said. "Certainly not to force you."

"Brother, I know what my duty is. My father chose this family to marry into so that we could bring about peace between our cities – Camelod and Rome – and between our two civilisations. I have always known that this was my role and I don't just accept it – I'm proud of it. It is not for us to choose or own way romantically as royals. Not even for you..."

"Nevertheless, I shall pester you day by day until I leave this city." I said, and I remember how she waved at me backwards as we walked away from each other – me filled with relief, and with hardly a hint of foreboding. Yet I never saw her alive again.

**

I am old now and I have seen many terrible and wonderful things in my life, but none have stayed with me like that vision of Imogen skipping away – as it turned out, to her death.

It is a mental picture that gave me the anger I needed to carry on fighting when all seemed lost, and the empathy I needed to understand the way people hope for the best sometimes when they are right to hope, and sometimes when there is none. At the time, that afternoon, seeing her so happy with married life raised my spirits. It wasn't exactly that I put side my fears, but I relaxed and returned to my other intractable problem – how to confirm or otherwise the intelligence I had stumbled upon during the wedding perhaps a week or so before.

It was this, I must accept, that was predominantly on my mind as I retraced my step towards Imogen's new husband's new home some evenings later, together with Verkingor and Divisiac, with whom I had been spending much of my time. To my surprise, as we arrived, two slaves – both white-faced with panic – came running past us. The rest of the household appeared to be running in all directions too. For a moment, we could get no sense out of them.

"What is going on? Where can I find my sister?" I asked one of them, a woman who I recognised, and was disconcerted when she sobbed in front of me and ran away. Even then, I had no fears. It was only when I turned around and saw Julius's father, the general, approaching me with his arms outstretched towards me that I realised something serious must have happened to her.

"My dear Caractacus," he began. "What can I say? I am at your service. I will do whatever you require."

"What? I don't understand. Has something happened?"

He blanched as he realised I had not been told. I could see Verkingor fingering his dagger in its sheath.

"It is your sister, I'm afraid. An accident. I fear to tell you…," he stammered. "She is dead."

I forgot myself at that moment and have no memory of the rest of our conversation. I could not believe that the girl I had entrusted to his son had been killed, even when I feared the worst.

"What kind of accident?" asked Divisiac, next to me.

"How? I don't understand it?"

"How, you ask?" The general looked desperate. "And will answer - both you and the gods. I believe there was an argument…"

I could barely believe what I was hearing.

"What? Then it is true! He killed her – your son killed her! Where is he now? Where is *she*?"

The general was, I know, an upright man - though he was to be responsible for horrors in my own country. Even so, I have never seen a man brought so low as I did at that moment, in the depth of his shame."

"I do not know," he said simply. "I just don't know."

"Let me see her."

I confess that I wept when I saw her body and the bruises on her head and neck, and the marks of the blow to the head which must have killed her. I have never seen such injuries before and never have since, though I have been in many battles and seen many wounds. It was not the horror of the blood so much as seeing her, who I loved, so broken.

I kissed her tenderly on her alabaster brow, as she lay there on the couch. I remembered my two companions, suddenly, and turned and saw them weeping too.

"Where is Gwalchmai?" I asked, remembering her bodyguard who I knew had still been with her. I feared the worst already.

"Alas…," said the general spreading his hands.

"Calm!" I said to Verkingor, who I saw reaching again for his weapon. "We must get out of here alive if we can and take the news home."

"And so," I said, now in cold fury. "What justice can I expect here? For I will have some…"

It was only at that moment that I realised the room was filling up with people, officials and servants, slaves and soldiers. I judged my chances of fighting my way out, tempted - as I never had been before - of dying there beside her body.

"Please don't insult me by offering me compensation," I said hastily as a man with a clipboard and tablet approached me.

I watched the general and his lawyer exchange glances. Then I stood by Imogen's battered body watching the general slip away.

"Make no mistake!" I shouted after him. "I will have my revenge on your son - in this world or the next! I came here in good faith and your son has murdered my sister and I will not forget his face…"

But he had gone.

"Listen, Prince Caractacus. You should not express yourself like that."

I stared at the lawyer in astonishment.

"What do you think? I should dance for joy?"

"By no means, Sir. My master, the general, has great admiration for you and he has asked me to give you some advice."

I bit my tongue for a moment, still weighing up whether we should rampage our way through the house in search of the man who was briefly my brother-in-law.

"You have – and everyone here has heard you do so – expressed a threat of revenge against the son of this house. Wait! Many might also understand why you did so. But what you have done is against our laws and customs in this city. And any more threats of revenge or reprisal will simply lead to your arrest and incarceration. You are a foreign visitor here – you can expect no protection from our laws…"

"What about my sister's husband. Are there no laws against what he has done?"

"I fear not," said the lawyer, increasingly smug. "I know there are some barbarian nations who fail to understand this, but we have strict laws of property in Rome. A man may dispose of his property as he wishes, and a wife is his property. That is civilisation."

"We shall see what history says about that," said Divisiac, quietly.

"Nevertheless. Let me be specific," said the lawyer, warming to his theme. "This house is now surrounded by soldiers who have been sent to take you into protective custody."

I fleetingly imagined again that the honourable course might be to face him down and to die fighting by the side of my sister. But I knew that would also lead to the deaths of my two companions. I also had another purpose – which was to get the urgent news to my father than the new emperor was planning an invasion.

"So what am I to do?" I asked, suddenly calm.

"We do not want trouble with Britain, certainly not so early in the reign of the Emperor Gaius. My master tells me that, if you will agree to leave quietly, then I am to conduct you out of the back door via a path, known only to the family, that will allow to you to avoid arrest."

I glanced round at Verkingor and Divisiac and saw them nodding assent.

"I have one further piece of advice for you, Prince Caractacus, if you value your life. Julius is a dangerous enemy and you must leave Rome. And don't leave by the Appian Way because he will find you there without difficulty."

"And if I were to appeal to the emperor?"

The lawyer looked at me patiently.

"Do you think Gaius will take your word over that of the Scapula family? I think not. Also, what you may not know about our new emperor…"

There was a commotion outside the door.

"Are we agreed?" he snapped. "Then follow me. And quickly…"

III - The kingdom by the sea

The clouds were rolling across the huge British sky and I could glimpse the sea in the distance – indeed I was so high on the Duns that I could see all the way to Vectis Isle. It was a beautiful spring morning and I had been home for some weeks and I felt the sunshine seeping into my bones and bringing me back to sanity and life. I badly needed it.

I had walked up from the temple on Changeburh Hill. At the old temple at the top, with its extraordinary view across the kingdoms, I had met an ancient retainer, who guided me across No Man's Land, down a narrow path which had once been wider, past wild brambles on either side and up, up to the old palace on the hill at Bryn Ciss.

My mission was to make contact with the old king of this peculiar seaside kingdom on behalf of my father and here was the difficulty: since Caesar's two fleeting visits a century before, the watchtowers that had warned of his arrival from these hills were overgrown and the high places undefended. What had been a tiny but powerful kingdom between the Duns and the sea, was now a mysterious and half-forgotten relic.

Yes, the King was still there, with his daughters, the descendents of those who had bravely provided the eyes of these islands and who had been over-run by the war-like Belgians when they had arrived, decades before I had been born. That was all I knew. My father had charged me with asking them if they might still be able to watch the sea for the expected Roman fleet.

He had wept for Imogen when I had told him the news, deeply ashamed that I had not shared her fate. But he had embraced me with such relief that I was still there with him that a little of that relief began to seep into me as well. Then he had raged, as I had, against the family of Scapula – and vowed revenge, powerless to achieve it, as I had been.

Even so, I had raged inwardly to myself for weeks after I had made my escape from Rome. I still find myself haunted by those images I brought with me.

I still remember the moment I had dodged back to kiss Imogen one last time on the forehead as the lawyer tapped his feet with increasing impatience and nervousness.

"They will expect you to leave by ship or to the south. I suggest you escape northwards through the Augustus Gate and find a ship at Alsium." He had been breathless by then as the four of us made it through the gardens and into the kitchens.

"Listen," I said, as I ran. "I will leave on one condition. That you will ask my druid friends at the druidic college to give my sister a proper funeral according to the rites of her people."

"You are in no position to set conditions, but I will make sure it is done. My master said you would expect nothing less."

We had reached a back gate past the buckets of slops beside the rear of the kitchen, and the lumps of fat and other detritus blocking the drains. The lawyer opened it and looked out carefully.

"It's clear. Go."

"Because, unlike you Romans, we all can expect an afterlife – not just emperors. That's what we believe…"

We both tried to catch our breath.

"Never mind that now," he said – "Do not fear, they are looking for one blond-haired Celt travelling alone, not three men. He handed me what looked very much like a dark wig. I put it on, then I pulled it straight off again.

"Never mind then - now go! GO!"

We strolled out into the street, trying to look inconspicuous, the Celtic prince, a warrior and a druid in this multi-faith, multinational and multi-roguish city.

We slipped through the Augustus Gate and bought three ponies from a dealer on the road and – by that evening – we were at sea, heading for Massilia and the trade routes north. It was only when we were on board, with the sea breeze in our hair, that I trusted myself to speak and to embrace my two companions and to weep for Imogen and Gwalchmai.

It was only then that I realised that Divisiac, being still with us, was coming too.

33

"I am coming with you, my prince," he said firmly.

"I am sorry. I have been so wrapped up in myself to realise."

"No matter. I too will wash the stench of a truly uncivilised city when I get home. I will write from Marsillia and instruct my colleagues what remains to be done. It will be an honour to be with you and to sing the songs of you, your sister and your courage."

"Courage? I don't think so," I said.

"There is courage in self-sacrifice and courage also in knowing when such gestures are futile. Courage too in realising instantly what is most important."

"I hope you are right. Please will you say the same to Verkingor?" I gestured to where my despairing bodyguard, an Atrebatian, was slumped by the gunwale.

"I have done and will do again."

I looked back towards the coast as it began to disappear. The sea breeze cooled my face as the misery and rage took hold. I looked back towards the great uncivilised dunghill that is Rome, past the cypress trees in the distance and vowed that – God forgive me – when I returned, I would be revenged on Julius Publius Scapula.

So I set out on my new and unexpected life as a fugitive. It is a life I have had to become used to since then.

**

It was when I was led across No Man's Land to the huge palace of Ciss, looming out of the mists at dawn, that I date the second moment that changed my life. I caught sight of the princess the moment I stepped across the threshold.

It is vouchsafed to few of us to love and find attractive the same person, and even fewer of us to hold that same person in their arms. But it has been to me and I thank God for it. Heaven knows, I had little thought, at that moment, that I was about to find love.

In recent years, I knew that my father's relations with Brigantia had cooled somewhat. I supposed I had still been contracted to Cartimandua, but thanks to divisions over policy at the Brigantian court, no further mention of her - or the contract between us - passed my father's lips. Of course I could hardly forget the erotic link between us that we had forged in Osen, and there will be those who criticise me for my failure to stand by my first love - and everything that followed from it. All I can say is that I believe I was led that day by God to Ciss.

So yes, I saw her across the huge chamber we had entered, Verkingor and myself. She had eyes that seemed to burn through me and the authority of intelligence. I had been involved of course with women since my encounter that night with Cartimandua, but none had that sense of erotic power that comes paradoxically through spiritual intelligence. For the first time since Imogen's murder and my humiliating retreat from Rome, I felt a leap of excitement about life and the world.

"Who is that beautiful woman?" I asked Verkingor.

"Sorry, my lord - I see none…"

Verkingor's failure to see what I saw brought me briefly to my senses. I also needed to complete my father's mission to see whether the quiet rulers of this kingdom by the sea might rearm its forts enough to watch over the channel of sea that divides us from Gaul, as they had done so successfully when Caesar had arrived some eighty or ninety winters or so before.

It crossed my mind again that it was strange that, having destroyed their multiple fortifications, the Belgians had never settled here. They used the old kingdom as a gateway to Britain that it was always designed not to be. They had settled instead around Venta Belgae and made it their home.

It was extraordinary, in fact, that there still appeared to be a functional palace here, let alone this princess who smiled at me, who led me down a long corridor with huge trees growing inside it and foliage. She still smiled but she was reticent about answering the many questions I asked as we walked beside her.

"Prince Caradoc," she said. "I am taking you to my father and he will give you answers, I am sure."

"I'm just asking about all these people here - where are they from?"

"They are just our patients. Peace be on your house and on your family."

There are some men, I am sure, who would have found this kind of reticence irritating, and so off-putting. There was something in her quiet intelligence that reminded me of Imogen. Perhaps that is what I had seen across that enormous and, as I had realised by then, relatively crowded room. What was it the first made me stare at her? Was it her olive skin and haunting eyes? Was it her elusive mystery or that glint in her eye which I was later to love?"

"You have met my daughter, Sarah, I see."

Until that moment, I had been unaware of the King's presence, dressed like a druid priest. I bowed low. Verkingor was on his knees in a moment.

With great humanity and modesty, the King bent down and lifted him up.

"Sarah? That is a ...?"

"A Jewish name? Yes it is?" said the King. "Because here in this kingdom by the sea, we trace our descent from Jewish merchants and seafarers who came here many, many winters ago. We are a product of our heritage, Prince Caradoc. Although we have lost our role, after the Belgians came, as the defenders of the coast – we are no longer warlike – we have continued our tradition of healing. We no longer study war."

I felt I had to reply to this.

"Sir," I said. "You know why I have come? I believe you must do. Tomorrow, if you are willing to discuss with me, I will attempt to persuade you to work with us to revive your historic role. Because the Romans are coming. Not today or tomorrow, maybe not for a few years - but they will come. And with your help, we want to be ready for them..."

"So that is the request from the High King, your father?" said the King, but he was interrupted by his daughter.

"And how will you stop them when they come?"

This must be Sarah herself. I felt myself struck suddenly dumb in her presence. I struggled to find the right word, any words.

"Princess Sarah, we will stop them the only way we can – to prevent them from landing."

"You mean that, once they have landed, they cannot be beaten?"

"I don't say that," I said, a little defensively. "Only that the Roman army has ridden roughshod over most of the known world and our best chance still remains the sea. But we don't know where they will land – wherever it is, this must be a possible place to stop them. That is why we need, at least to man your old lookout points from your old strongholds, so we can get the early warnings we need to win. That is how my ancestor Cassivelaun beat Caesar so long ago."

"I am glad," she said, her smile once more lighting up her face. "I am glad that, although you are prince and a warrior, you are prepared to speak of your military plans to me as if I was an equal. Not all warriors, perhaps even few of them, would do that."

"Well, I..." I was unsure how to reply. "You may not know that my mother was a warrior. We Camelod people do these things differently, at least to the Romans!"

She laughed then and, in that moment, the trees around us seemed to put out more foliage and I wanted her. Perhaps, even from that stage, I loved her – and I knew I had not loved before.

It was a nervous moment because I knew the kingdom by the sea was in the front line should the new emperor – the one the Romans knew as Caligula – choose to come that way. I would have to find a way to protect her.

**

In the three days I spent among the strange vegetable palace of Bryn Ciss, I spent some hours with the King, asking him whether he might be prepared to reinstate his day and night watch which I begged him to consider for the sake of the nation in the face of invasion. When I was not doing that, I sought out Sarah and asked her to show me around her father's tiny realm.

She did so just from Bryn Ciss. She took me to the ramparts that defended the hill on the northern side, all broken and battered, the stones which had formed the basis for defence scattered away down the hillside.

"I know what you have been asking my father," she told me. "I also know what it will cost him to answer you. You must understand that, although we may be able to act again as look-outs, we can't any more re-fortify and man these defences. I mean, how could we, even with enough warriors?"

"What if I could supply the warriors?" I asked hopefully.

She stared ruefully out to sea.

"Even then. Even then, we have built up such an expertise with our patients, those with maladies of the mind, with overwhelming melancholia. We use a combination of the love of God, the peace of Christ and a small flower that grows only on chalk – which, as you must have seen, we have here in abundance. Perforate wort, we call it. And it works. We have dedicated our work and this place to the sacred memory of John, the brother of Our Lord…"

I felt confused. It was the first time I had heard this language.

"I'm sorry, Sarah. I feel lost – who is this lord you speak of?"

I never heard her answer – if indeed she gave one. Because at that moment, a messenger ran up to us and fell on his knees beside my companion.

Sarah lifted him up. "My lady Sarah," he said, panting. "I have a message for your guest."

"What is your message?" I said, attempting to sound encouraging.

"It is sad news and I dare not say, my lord."

"You must say," said Sarah, firmly.

"It is about your father," said the servant, addressing me but looking appealingly at her. "He was thrown from his horse some days ago and a messenger has arrived from your brother asking you to return home as fast as you can."

My jaw gaped in horror.

I confess that there had been little love lost between my

father and myself. I was very glad, relieved even, to have been included in his councils a little after Imogen's death, and for the strategy which he shared with me, but my first thought was not for him – it was for the nations of Britain. This was a terrible moment to lose a High King, with the Romans camped on the other side of the sea, as I now understood that they were.

**

I had realised my father must be injured as I rode home and Verkingor and myself kicked our horses forward, just as I kicked myself for saying so little to Sarah about what I felt and whether and where we might meet again. I had taken enough time to conclude with her father his agreement to mount look-outs at Bryn Ciss and the other high points along his narrow realm, and to light the old beacons along this stretch of the coast if the Roman fleet was ever sighted. But I had concluded nothing with his daughter.

I had little idea of what she might or might not have felt about me.

"Farewell, my friend," she had said. "May Christ be with you."

It was not a farewell I had ever heard before at that stage of my life. In the days that followed, as I hurried by ship to Trinovan and then by horse again to Camelod beyond, I thought of her increasingly, and her lonely life tending the herbs and the wretched of mind and body on Bryn Ciss.

I knew this was not helping me. The Roman emperor Gaius was perhaps even then marching north with his legions. And along with my brother, and my father as High King, I shared in the responsibility for holding him back.

When I reached the city gates, I found a dishevelled Togod waiting for me. I had never seen him look so relieved to see me

"You are welcome, brother," he said. "But you are too late. Our father died last night."

IV - Togod

"He died?

"I am afraid so."

We hugged each other. We had lived in the shadow of our mighty father for so long that it seemed impossible to grasp that it had in fact happened.

I was also aware that we were in a dangerous situation ourselves. There was, after all, a long British tradition of fratricide when it came to the transfer of power. But Togod could not doubt my loyalty. Could he?

"You will be King," I said as clearly, loudly and unambiguously as I could.

I had always loved my brother, even during the difficult period that lay ahead. I love him now, though we have not seen each other in the flesh for three decades. I never resented the fact that he had been born a few minutes before me so that he received all the attention. In some ways, he had faced the more difficult childhood or preparation. He had not been betrothed to anyone, let alone spent the night between Cartimandua's extraordinary thighs.

Even so, I was relieved when we fell into each other's arms. And it was clear that he was relieved as well.

"Thank you, Caradoc. I will need you in the years to come. Especially now that the Roman armies are waiting just across the Narrow Sea.

"They are here?" I was alarmed.

"Well, not yet, but we have to assume they will be sailing soon. I heard from our people in Trinovan that there are two legions on the coast of Gaul awaiting the arrival of the Emperor."

My mind froze for a moment. Surely we should be doing more than discussing the succession. What a time for my father to remove himself to the afterlife!

Togod must have read my thoughts.

"Poor Cunobelin. He must be cross at having to miss all this.

After all his preparations and diplomacy.

We both laughed rather sadly, aware that we would have to conjure up some of our father's aura of power and capability.

"Is it not time to call the great council together?" I asked.

"Yes, but although I may be King, I am not yet the High King. Only the council can decide such matters but only the High King can call the council. Still, there are procedures and we are putting them in place."

Throughout this conversation, I had been doing my sums. The legions were camping on the other side of the Narrow Sea between us and the Roman world. If they were really waiting for the Emperor, then they would not leave without him – but the hard fact was that he could already be here. We might have a couple of weeks at the most to plan and prepare.

"We can't wait for procedures," I said. "You must call the other rulers to you. That is clear and, if possible, in two weeks from now. Faster if possible. We have very little time."

Togod's eyes narrowed and, for a moment, I wondered if I had been too outspoken. The brothers of kings need sometimes to learn to bite their tongues. But whatever had clouded his mind passed in a moment, and he was agreeing with me. Even so, I promised myself to be a little more careful.

**

All the way home, along the voyage around the coast to Trinovan and the old roads beyond it, I puzzled over the issue of love. I had no doubt in my mind that I loved the princess Sarah. Something about her combination of reticence or shyness and directness had captured my heart. I loved her.

But what was I to do about my long betrothal to Cartimandua in the north? We had spent a night of passion together, which is more than I could say of Sarah, though it had been some years before and - although I thought of her often - I never felt the compelling sense that I now did with Sarah.

I knew, of course, that to break my betrothal would be a serious act of public betrayal – especially, as I now knew, my father was dead and we needed our alliances as never before. What was I to do?

**

"We should let the facts be known widely across the realm," said Fidelma. She was clearly becoming a valued advisor since Cunobelin's death. She was at least a generation older than me, and she always seemed to know the right solutions to suggest.

I repeated what she said. We needed a council of rulers, and we were best placed to call it.

I forget now when the news arrived that the Emperor had asked his legionaries to pick up shells on the beach before sending them home. It seemed to us when we heard it that the report could not have been entirely accurate – it could not have been, or so I thought at the time. Later, as it became clear that it had been true, the optimists among us comforted themselves that our will to resist might be strengthened. It was clear that, if they had got as far as the beach, then they would undoubtedly try again soon, on some pretext or other.

The confirmation that the Emperor Gaius, known to history as 'Little Boots', was really only interested in shells – and that, this time at least, we had nothing to fear, came at the most inconvenient moment possible for us. Just as the gathering of kings had gathered around the great round table of Camelod, and just as they were nodding their grave agreement to our collective plans for our defence of Albion.

The news had arrived as our guests did, from all over Britain. From the south, my father's old enemy, King Verica of Atrebatia, venturing across the Thames to make sure Cunobelin was really dead. He looked ancient and not entirely sane, with long grey hair, unpleasantly unwashed, across his face. He was muttering something to himself something which could have been curses, and probably were.

From the north, standing in for Cardimandua's father was a vast local magnate called Venutis, an anti-Roman firebrand from Brigantia. From Icenia in the east came King Esuprast, who came with his striking red-haired daughter Boudicca, who I could not help staring at. Venutis looked familiar for some reason I could not quite place.

From the west came the king of Siluria, my cousin Arvir. He took me aside after he arrived. "Cousin Caradoc," he said. "I know not why the Romans *say* they are coming, but take it from me: I know the real reason."

"Really? How do you know?"

"And it has nothing to do with revenge for our defeat of Julius Caesar," he said, ignoring me. "Or our tin mines or silver production. Or because they want to suppress the way our men and women live equal lives."

"So, what is it then?"

"It is because of the Way. The new religion from Palestine, because it threatens the way the Romans live. That is why – and because some of the main adherents have taken shelter here in Britain."

"How do you know this?"

"Because I have met them and I have given them land in Siluria."

Arvir sounded triumphant.

"Well, perhaps we should ask them to leave again – at least until we can be certain we can defend ourselves..?"

He breathed deeply.

"That is why I am just telling you, Caradoc. You will meet them too, I feel sure. Then you will know why I cannot do so."

I remembered the conversation later, but at the time, I am afraid, I did not take him seriously.

But as he greeted these arrivals, I saw Togod grow in confidence and stature and, I have to say, I was delighted. He had never been one to stick to a plan before, because – with a father like ours – he tended to lack confidence in his own ideas. I knew that my father's attention, for which I had been jealous of Togod, had not always been so welcome.

I told him this after the first council session. "Thank you, Caradoc," he said. "It is true that father was tougher on me than he was on you – which is why I was jealous of you. I wanted the freedom you were allowed. He wanted me to rule like he had and then it is already difficult to rule like me."

It occurred to me then that what may have looked like freedom to him looked more like neglect to me.

"How do you mean?" I asked.

"I mean I will not be doing any mass executions. For any reason whatever. Nor, despite Verica being the most irritating old curmudgeon you might ever hope to meet, will I be leading raids against the Atrebates any more."

At least Verkingor would be pleased.

"What will you do then?"

"What? As if there was nothing to kingship apart from raids and executions - and druid ritual?" He laughed.

"No, I mean, how will King Togod rule?"

He looked away across the forests outside the city.

"Caradoc, there is a more urgent question we have to answer. Who do we want to be high king after my father? To lead our forces in battle?"

"You mean we should accept somebody from outside our family?"

"I am just asking. What is your advice? You're my chief advisor – so *advise…*"

**

We had already asked ourselves the question, in fact. When the point arrived in the proceedings of that first national conference of British kings that we needed to discuss who would lead us in battle, I could see old Verica stirring and feared the worst.

We had discussed our tactics if the Romans should land in Cant, south of the Thames, and agreed that it would be sensible to hold back – if we could not meet them where they landed – we would make our stand on the north bank of the river and overwhelm them when they were half way across.

"You would hand over my whole country to the Romans to do with as you see fit?" Verica shouted, his face red and apoplectic with rage. "You … you … would harry my borders until your own go down to the north bank of the great river,

then you just abandon everyone that is left behind to their fate
- and YOU!" He leapt to his feet and pointed at the other kings
around the table. "You are so pathetic that you let them do it.
If that's your attitude to defending us, I want none of it...!"

He harrumphed and cursed until he had left the room. We
could all hear him cursing as he stepped with his few
supporters into the courtyard outside.

V - Defection and defence

Nervous about what old Verica might do - aware that it could be practically anything - I sent intermediaries to Calleva to try to intervene. I knew he probably had not very long to live and I was hardly surprised when his son-in-law took the reins of Atrebatia.

It is worth putting on record here that, despite my pleasure that he was no longer the king there, I had nothing to do with what the old curmudgeon later described as a 'coup'. Neither, as far as I knew, did Togod - though it was us, the sons of Cunobelin - that he was later accusing of stealing his throne.

That was all later, after my brother's first winter on the throne. Aware that the Emperor could try again the following year, I had been tightening our diplomatic links with the kingdoms of Britain, aware of all the preparations for invasion that were taking place, and as part of this role, I managed other visits to Sarah and the Kingdom by the Sea.

I also knew that Cartimandua's father and elder brother had both died over the previous months and that she was now the Queen of the Brigantia. It might have been sensible now, if I could really subsume my own passions to my nation's needs, to renew our relationship and to marry her. But I knew - because everyone did - that she had also courting the local magnate called Venutis. Perhaps that was what the Brigantian nobles insisted on if they were to accept a queen. They were famously conservative in such matters.

Also, I felt no yearning for her. Quite the reverse, in fact, since I had met Sarah in the tiny but defensively critical Kingdom by the Sea. It was now Sarah I dreamed about at night, awake and asleep, and when very occasionally I could persuade some woman into my bed. I had all but forgotten Cartimandua, as she must have known the moment she saw me across the huge conference room in Osen - the very last place we had glimpsed each other.

The kings met in conference there a second time, also at

Beltane, having heard about the fate of the Emperor Gaius - murdered by his own bodyguard some winters later. Our intelligence suggested he was incapable of leading any kind of military operation. That was also what our informants has said of his successor, Claudius, who - because of his deafness and a range of other disabilities - had not been considered a threat to either of the homicidal barbarians who had preceded him in office. But they quickly changed their minds and through this next winter - after we had discovered Verica's defection to Rome - we agreed to hold a great council again at Osen. Claudius was coming. There was little doubt.

I am sure, knowing the sharpness of this Emperor's mind, that he immediately dismissed Verica as senile, when he arrived begging for Roman support to regain the throne of Atrebatia. But this was clearly a useful pretext. I bitterly condemned myself for my failure to build bridges via my neighbouring cousin King Guider in Siluria. Looking back, it seems unlikely that Claudius would have restrained himself even without Verica.

Still, the choice of Osen was partly to avoid such mistakes in the future. It was outside all kingdoms and factions.

So there we sat, Togod and I, in our blue cloaks pinned to our right shoulders, like the other British nobles, men and women, those from Dumnonia in their green cloaks, the Dutroges in their yellow ones and those from Icenia in their brown ones. I could not help staring again at old King Esuprast and his daughter, younger than me and with striking good looks. It was only then that I first heard her name.

"Who is that beauty next to the king in the Iceni delegation?" I asked Verkingor, standing beside me.

"Oh, that is Boudicca, I believe. The heir to King. She is wonderful, isn't she?"

"She might be too wonderful," said Divisiac. "She looks absolutely terrifying."

There also, I suddenly caught sight of Cartimandua with her delegation and a huge man next to her, who I took to be her new betrothed. When they had settled themselves in the Brigantes' usual place, I recognised him. It was indeed

Venutis who had represented them at Camelod.

I could see her scanning the room too, and guessed - a little immodestly perhaps - that she was seeking me out.

Our eyes met. She winked.

I felt oddly nervous. Queens do not, in my experience, wink without some reason. Even new ones.

There was little time to worry too much because, as the senior monarch - the son of the High King - Togod was on his feet outlining the situation.

"Peoples of Albion!" he said. "I greet you, and - though I may be too young yet to take the place of my dear, dead father - I am claiming the right as son of the High King to steer the proceedings this morning. Do you agree?"

There were murmurs around the table. The druid high priest Bran nodded firmly, and rose to bless us.

"Thank you, Bran," said Togod at the end of the ritual. "Blessings be upon you as well."

My brother now rose to his feet and paced around the outside of the room, forcing some of the delegations to crane their heads around to see him.

"We have come for many miles some of us, from the icy realms of the far north to the sea cities and lake towns of the west, to be here today and this critical moment in our history. We know that, once more, the Romans are coming. We believe that three legions have been ordered from their bases on the River Rhine to gather on the north coast of Gaul, from where they will await their orders to sail."

"And the weather!" shouted an obviously drunken member of the delegation from the Belgian city of Caer Venta.

"And the weather indeed, probably our greatest ally," said Togod. "Either way, we are here to discuss our response to this - whether to fight, what tactics to use, and above all, who should lead us at this moment. My great-grandfather Cassivelaun certainly believed we should intercept them on the beaches as they land, if that is at all possible. It would be extremely hard to co-ordinate. I believe that may still be the best policy, but I didn't want to prejudice your discussion, so - the floor is yours…"

He looked around the gathering expectantly.

"I recognise the Queen of Brigantia."

To my surprise, Cartimandua was on her feet - surprised because I had expected some of the older warriors to speak first and because I knew - I remembered - that she actually wanted some kind of permanent arrangement that would link us all with the Roman world.

"Thank you, King Togod. I wanted to be the first to speak, not just so that we might welcome each other to our respective thrones, but also to plead for negotiation - although this is not the agreed position of my own delegation, I accept. I believe we should be careful not to become slaves of the Romans by resisting and then failing. By all means, let us fight to begin with - if they land this time. What I am saying is that, whether or not we have the will, we don't have the *means* to resist if it is their intention to launch a full-scale invasion..."

I was impressed. She could really speak. She seemed to have grown in stature since our last encounter. Judging by the shuffling around the room, this was not universally shared.

"Sit down, you witch!"

That was unnecessary, I frowned at the Silurian delegation, from where the barracking had emerged.

"Please, please," said Togod, a little desperately. "Let us remember our great traditions of plain speaking here. We need honesty, now of all time. Does anyone agree with the Queen of Brigantia?"

It was hardly surprising that the Belgian delegation from the south raised their hands. I was more surprised to see that the Icenis did the same, but I remembered their close trading relationships with the Romans and realised I should not have been.

The Atrebates were clearly in some confusion. I felt sure their new rulers would hardly want the Romans to return Verica to their throne. But the two from Trinovan also raised their hands.

"And of you that agree, which of you will go along with the majority and send soldiers, contribute to the fighting, if such a decision is made here? So - we have four of our nations at least, and possibly five…" He glanced at the Atrebates. "…who are in favour of some kind of negotiated settlement…"

"No!" shouted a large Brigantian next to Venutis. "Never, never, never!"

I saw him nodding approvingly. It would be hard to see how those two would ever be successfully married, I thought to myself - deciding in my own mind that Cartimandua and Venutis would never be wed.

"Let us hear some other opinions," Togod was saying. I could see Fidelma whispering in his ear, presumably suggesting who he should ask to speak. "We have, let me be precise, three of our rulers in favour, four if you count Verica, plus Trinovan."

It was clear to me, and presumably to Fidelma, that - unless more suddenly decided they were in favour of immediate negotiations, then the day would soon be won for total defiance. I began to feel a distinct kind of relief. There was nobody from the tiny Kingdom by the Sea, though I had sent messages asking Sarah if she might come herself, which meant we still had eight delegations - plus the nation of druids - and a clear majority in favour of resistance.

In fact, I was unsure which side Sarah would be on.

It was mainly trading nations that most wanted peace, and were prepared to accept Roman rule, almost no matter what, but the western traders had been expected to break ranks. The Durotrigians around the trading port of Hengistbury argued for peace and, when the southern Silurians suggested a less confrontational approach, I began to get nervous.

"Let us at least talk to the new Emperor," a Dumnonian was saying. "I believe he is not entirely monstrous. I feel sure he would prefer to avoid bloodshed if possible. Let us at least send a delegation now to Rome to hear his terms."

"No!" I shouted, leaping to my feet. And more quietly, I said to Togod: "May I speak now?"

"I recognise my brother, Prince Caradoc of Camelod," he said.

This was my only opportunity to swing the British nations behind resistance, I believed. I had to make it count. I looked around the room, at the expectant faces, most of whom I knew, but the sight gave me energy.

"No," I said again. "You can't negotiate with a lion when it is preparing to spring. It makes no sense. If we can stand firm, I believe we can protect everything that is most important about the way we live here. We must be in no doubt: if the Romans come, then they come for slaves and booty. I have been in Rome - I know the real reasons they come. They cannot abide a more civilised nation on their borders. We live in equality between our womenfolk and our menfolk. They *own* their wives as they do their sheep and their donkeys - that is how I lost my lovely sister Imogen to their cruelty, as many of you will know. We live in small communities and linked farms that provide for our needs; their cities starve the countryside. We have servants who are free to come and go; they have slaves. We hold to the ancient wisdom of the druid and worship the one God; they worship bulls or statues or their own emperors. We cannot allow our beautiful land to come under their domination."

I paused for effect, to let these words sink in. I glanced over at Cartimandua and unfortunately she saw me and repeated her wink. I stared for a second before remembering what I had planned to say.

"Yes, if they were to come here and to exert their power over us, some few of us would be richer as a result. Yes, a few of us might enjoy underfloor heating and circus games. But many of us would ourselves be slaves in their great houses or starving in their new cities. That is why we must unite to fight them. They believe that their might makes them right. Our continued existence, free from tyranny or poverty, means that there remains some hope that they can't spread their malign influence over the whole world."

There was a cheer from various parts of the hall and I stood back and I sat down, exhausted. I glanced over to the Brigantes group; Venutis was among those cheering. Cartimandua, next to him, was not. She was staring in my direction with a knowing smile across her face. I felt sure I had failed again to convince her.

**

By the time the conference had finished, and the various royal parties were heading for their long journey home, we had made progress. Togod had been appointed our leader in battle, which was one step from taking our father's place as High King. I could see how pleased Fidelma was with the outcome.

We had even hammered out and agreed our tactics – on the appointed signal that the legions were massing on the coast of Gaul, then our allies would send their armed contributions to a combined army at Camelod and wait for the Romans to land, where the men and women of Cant would try to prevent their landing. Once they had bypassed this, and had reached the banks of the Thames, we would intercept them and tackle them when they were half way across. We could then use our chariots, and our superior knowledge of the area, to best effect.

I was clearing my head from the intensity of the day, wondering about these tactics from every angle, and horribly aware of the opposition, when I met Cartimandua again. We had both been walking along the river at its narrowest point, towards the docks at Osenford - in the gathering twilight. She refrained from her previous aloofness and I noticed that she held my face as we kissed.

"That was a pretty speech, my betrothed," she said, a little challengingly.

"I understood you were now betrothed elsewhere." I confess that I was a little taken aback.

"Ah yes, but in my heart it will always be you, Caradoc."

She was still smiling. Was she teasing me or was she serious? I could not tell from her smile, but we laughed a little at the impossibility of such an idea.

"I fear your advisors would not allow me to marry you now you are Queen. Queens can only marry kings, at least if they are going outside their own borders. You know I am right."

"Maybe - but I see no reason why we should not meet sometimes. As we're doing now. So. Come with me now, Prince Caradoc. I command you."

She laughed flirtatiously and I was suddenly on my guard again. I certainly did not want to end up as some kind of captured prize, a pawn in the Brigantian great game.

"I tell you what," I said. "Come with me to the end of the forest over there, past the cattle." I pointed towards a few cows who chewed in the half-light beside the forest. "Come with me where we can still be as equal as we were once before."

I must confess I found myself stirred to see Cartimandua again but, I had Sarah on my mind, and the understanding I felt I had with her, and the Kingdom by the Sea.

I decided to tell her, and her face clouded.

"Betrayer," she said, grinning haughtily. "So we are *both* betrothed elsewhere."

"Yes," I said, "but, if I am to be completely honest, my heart is taken too."

She was silent for a while.

"You mean to say - we are no longer lovers?"

"We are perhaps friends in a way that only former lovers can be. You will always be special to me, Cartimandua."

"Yes," she said, simply. And so we sat and talked until darkness had covered us, about Rome and its virtues and vices and the future and our respective marriages and whether they would ever happen. Her feelings about Venutis, the huge man I had seen disagreeing with her at the conference, were divided in the extreme. I told her about my fears for the future and whether I would survive an encounter with the Roman army. We held hands as we talked.

When we could no longer see the river from our hiding place, she got to her feet and kissed me.

"I must go. Queens are not allowed to be alone for very long."

"That is their tragedy," I said. "But in your case, it seems to be an important element of the future."

"Go well then, my love," she said. "Only make sure, Prince Caradoc, that you never find yourself alone in Brigantia. That's all I can say."

I took that back then as mere banter, with some innuendo, but I may have been wrong. In retrospect, as events were to take shape, she may perhaps have meant it.

VI - The landings

"We must suppress this news," I told Togod in somewhat arrogant terms. "If it spreads, our army will begin to drift away, especially when we get to harvest time."

"But how can we?" said Fidelma. "The news will seep out and will undermine the trust of our allies."

The news was that the Roman army, camped on the coast of Gaul, was refusing to cross the sea – for reasons we could not quite understand. Yes, of course, we could fall back on bravado and say they were frightened of us but, in our heart of hearts, we knew this was unlikely. I saw that Fidelma was right - the last thing we wanted to do was to foster a false sense of confidence. Military planning relies, above all else, on being able to see clearly - as I was slowly learning.

So what could we do?

I had visions of what leaders like King Guider would be saying to his commanders when he heard the news. Even so, I saw a shadow over the brow of my brother and, perhaps for the first time, I saw that he was cross with me. His forehead seemed to bulge as it did when he was angry.

"Oh Caradoc, you are so certain about everything - why can't you see there are shades of grey? Don't you think this news will actually give our armies courage? It shows that ordinary Roman soldiers are nervous about meeting us in battle."

"If it's true, it might…"

"*If* it's true? Do you have some reason to doubt it?"

"I don't doubt it. Not now - all I'm saying is that it might not *stay* true…" I was unsure whether to reveal my sources, even to my brother, aware that it could lead to awkward conversations about Sarah and the Kingdom by the Sea. I had no idea where she was getting her information from either. I had hardly spent enough time there to ask, after all.

"No, and please don't take that aggressive tone with me, Caradoc. I am not just your twin brother. I am the King and you and Fidelma here are my chief advisors."

I bowed to him in deference, something I had hardly ever done before, and certainly not when we were almost alone. And as I did so, I realised that there might be another difficult conversation we should perhaps have now, since he was already cross with me.

"On another matter…"

"Yes," said Togod, visibly changing gear. I realised his position was ageing him quickly.

"I believe there is a Roman spy in Camelod. Or at least a military plant. More than that, I believe I know who it is – I thought it was my fevered imagination when I caught sight of him myself, and then he saw me too - and he skipped away into the market crowd. As well he might."

"If you mean Scapula, then you are right. He has been here. And before you say anything, Caradoc, I know his significance. I know what he did to our sister."

"You *know*? And yet you…" I was getting angry now myself.

"Yes, yes. *Listen!*" Togod was struggling to control himself. He checked outside the hall in case there was anyone listening.

"Because I am the King. I will be the High King. Britain stands or falls by *my* decisions, not yours. I have responsibilities you don't understand for some reason. Yes, I loved my sister – *our* sister. But I need to put my own private feelings and jealousies and rivalries to one side occasionally, and this is one of those occasions."

Then he strapped on his swordbelt and stormed out, leaving Fidelma and myself staring uncomfortably at each other.

"And don't ever accuse me of failing to live up to my responsibilities again," he shouted as he disappeared outside.

"He is uncertain what to do for the best," said Fidelma. "That is difficult for a king, but especially when he must not show it."

I knew what she meant.

"Of course," I said, not entirely truthfully. "How many times have I thanked the one God that he was born first and not me."

**

It was later that same day, or perhaps a day later, I remember, that I received my first proper letter addressed to me from Sarah. It was brought to me by a strange woman with long grey hair, dressed in the garb of a druidic priest.

She came to me out of the shadows in the royal hall in Camelod and, although we recognised each other, wordlessly she handed me a piece of parchment wrapped in a cloth.

I took it straight back to my chamber, where I could be relatively alone, and unwrapped it. This is what it said.

"From Sarah of Bryn Ciss to Prince Carodoc of Camelod, greetings in Christ.

As I write this, my faithful Oonag awaits me with a swift horse, ready to speed this to you, my love.

She does so because we have seen the Roman fleet, maybe eighty maybe a hundred ships of war sailing across the Narrow Sea to our coast, where they divided their forces. I have seen this with my own eyes. I have seen the sunlight glinting on their weapons. The beacons are lit. Even now, I hope, the soldiers of Cant are preparing for war.

As they approached the coast, the bulk of the fleet turned eastwards, heading I know not where. The smaller detachment of perhaps twenty ships turned westwards and I believe by their course they are heading for Vectis. My intention is to go now to the old temple on Changeburh Hill and watch their progress, and to see which way they go around the island.

May God be with you in whatever struggle ensues. My love will surround you too and I believe that, through Christ, we can keep you from harm.

Please write back quickly and tell me how things go with you.

Yours always in Christ."

My immediate reaction, I confess, was joy that Sarah had recognised me and my love and was returning it. It was a confirmation of the understanding between us that I believed was there but was never quite certain. There was also a new language which I did not at the time understand – "yours in Christ" meant little to me in those days.

But next reaction was excitement, tinged with fear, that what we had thought about and planned for ever since I could remember was now upon us. I felt sure we could win, as Cassivelaun had done against Julius Caesar, nearly ninety winters before. But where was Togod?

I asked Fidelma and she had no idea - or so she said. We had to assume he had left the palace halls. What should I do? I waited, pacing up and down with Fidelma, Divisiac and Verkingor for an hour, getting increasing nervous. Then two hours had passed.

"We must act," said Verkingor. "We must waste no more time before we tell the allies, as we promised we would. The news must be already four or five days old. They have probably already landed somewhere."

I cursed myself for failing to ask Sarah's grey-haired servant when she had left. Perhaps if we had not so recently disagreed so unexpectedly, I would have taken the initiative and acted on Togod's behalf, but I didn't want to alienate him further.

Also I had a nervous fear about where he had gone. If Scapula had really arrived to claim to be an honest broker, apparently advising but actually spreading some kind of defeatism - then there had to be some way to counteract his evil influence. But how could I if he would only meet Togod?

Yet, as we waited, the reports began to arrive. An exhausted messenger scrambled in to say he had seen soldiers landing on the Cantish coast near Dover. There had already been minor engagements, he said. But the main fleet had been sailing northwards towards the estuary of the Thames.

This was a potential problem. As my colleagues knew all too well, our preparations had been based on a landing south of the Thames. If the Romans were to land on the north bank, it would require an immediate change of tactics.

"And why do you think they have divided their forces?" I asked. "That does indeed seem strange."

"I could understand why they might decide to take Vectis

Isle," said Fidelma. "Perhaps as some kind of base or bridge to the mainland - especially given their public reason for being here, or so I understand it, is to restore old Verica to the throne in Atrebatia…"

We all began talking at once.

"So the fact that the main body of the invasion force was headed for our biggest trading city - to Trinovan and, presumably, north to Camelod implies that isn't a punitive expedition," I said. "Where *is* my brother."

The truth was I feared I knew where Togod was. I was afraid he was ensconced somewhere with the man who had murdered his sister. A man who was posing as an emissary from the Emperor but who had actually come to confuse and to lead astray. I looked at Fidelma and wondered if she feared the same thing. She nodded to me in a subtle way.

"I don't believe we can wait any longer," I said, feeling hugely relieved at having made the decision.

We walked quickly to the table beside the throne where the confirmatory orders to the different commanders, aware that that most of the kings would be with their soldiers. I signed them myself. The messengers were waiting and I watched them go, kicking their heels into the flanks and through the dust at the city gates and away. Our first move was now confirmed: we would gather at Homestead, overlooking Trinovan in the distance, from where we could watch an invading army on the march as it approached.

From that moment, there was a timetable to be kept. I had to be there myself in just two days, which was not long to travel as much as the Dumnonians, for example. I was aware that most of the army from Camelod had been there for weeks, but I would have to ready our final contingent. I had understood the ways of men enough to know that, as the nearest large city to the gathering pace, we would inevitably be less well-prepared than perhaps we should have been.

I scribbled a reply to Sarah as loving as I could make it within the boundaries of decency and sent it back. I had sent word to our watchers along the estuary coast to let us know, and to get into their positions. I had lit the fuse that would allow the watchers to communicate with our army on the march. What else was there to do before I climbed on my own horse and galloped through the gates after the army?

Of course. I needed to write a message for Togod, wherever he was, to tell him what had been done in his name, to beg his forgiveness and to promise to see him overlooking Trinovan with the rest of us.

VII - Invasion

To his day, I have little idea where my brother was during those first hours of the news of the invasion of our land. I fear that Scapula was weaving his web of lies, but who knows? I do not.

In any case, he arrived not long after I did at Homestead Hill, together with the King's bodyguard and his other advisors, who I had left behind searching for him around Camelod. He was strangely reserved and preoccupied when we met and I decided I would have to somehow find a moment to be alone with him.

"What is the matter with my brother?" I asked Fidelma.

"Oh, I don't know. He has been a little moody since we left Camelod. The hour hangs heavily on him, as it does on us all."

I realised she was completely exhausted.

"Can you rest now, Fidelma?"

"I could - but I daren't," she said, with an attempt at a smile.

As it was, the situation was changing so fast that none of us could really rest. There were also the predictable difficulties co-ordinating the different military forces we were supposed to meet there.

"Where are the troops from Dumnonia? Have they not arrived?"

"They've been here for weeks but I haven't seen them for some time," said Verkingor, who I had asked to make sure everyone was there and that they all sent senior people to liaise with us. "They are camped in a village not far from here to the west."

"And the Silurians? Where the hell are the Silurians. I expected some no-shows – I don't suppose they'll be joining us from Atrebatia – but has my cousins Guider or Arvir arrived…?"

There was an ancient burial mound on the summit of the hill and beside it, and respectfully to the east, we constructed a huge makeshift tent to meet the various commanders. Arvir arrived soon the next morning. There was Gwalchmai, the heir to the throne of Dumnonia. There was Venutis, my rival for the hand of Cartimandua, who had brought a small contingent of Brigantes. There was Beddwyr, the leader of the elite druid fighting force from Caer Leon.

"The main force follows shortly," Venutis told me. That was a relief. It was dark now and behind me and all around the slopes of the hill I could see the camp fires of our army. It all seemed calm, and even quite well-organised. I walked over to the mound, with the summer breeze on my face.

It was then that I realised why Venutis seemed familiar. It was the first time I had heard his voice and I had a moment of revelation that he had been the young man in a mask who had attacked me after the night I spent with Cartimandua, all those years before. So he had achieved his objective, at least – he now had the woman he had fought for in is bed.

I stared down towards the city in the distance, invisible now that the gloaming had turned to night. Somewhere beyond there, the Roman legions were on the march. Who was buried at this spot? What ancient high king of Albion or general perhaps at the place of some long-forgotten triumph? Would he have known what to do to guarantee the independence of our British kingdoms?

I did not know the answers to my own musings but I tried to sense the person in his grave and begged forgiveness for disturbing them in their sleep. But, if they wouldn't mind interceding on our behalf…

I looked over towards the fire we had lit outside the main tent and I could see an ancient and stooped figure there. For a moment my neck chilled suddenly as I wondered if the inhabitant of the tomb had really acceded to my request and risen from the dead. I dashed over.

"Who is this worthy old man?" I asked the sentry.

"He is from Brigantia, sir."

"Bring him to me…"

The ancient who I had taken for a ghost turned out to bring a necklace, a gift from Cartimandua. I was touched for a moment.

"I thank your Queen, sir. But did she also send an army?"

The old man bowed low.

"Alas, the army is not yet ready. She asks me to tell you that it will be here within sixteen days."

My heart sank.

No Brigantians, apart from Venutis's small band. That was all we needed. I imagined the Roman army, disciplined and cruel, their eagles swaying above them, marching north. Yes, we had the fact that we were defending our own homes and soil on our side, but would it be enough?

**

"I fear we are too few, brother," said a voice behind me as I entered the tent for our council the next morning. "We cannot be more than 7,000 here."

I am, I fear, an awkward man. So, suddenly, in the face of Togod's doubts, I felt suddenly more confident. It was a good thing I did, because I was supposed to open the proceedings that morning.

I stood and looked around the grizzled warriors, the commanders of the different elements in our hastily bundled together line of defence of our homes. Then I took a deep breath.

"No, we do not have the experience of war that the enemy has," I said, realising that I was also addressing the chiefs of staff, which explained the lines of crusty old warhorses around the room.

"But we have two elements that the Romans don't have – we are defending our lands, our homes, our families and what we believe. If we lose, we will lose everything - our freedom, our religion, our God, and we will live if we live to see our families sold into slavery. If we lose, the historians of the future will believe *we* were the barbarians. If they lose, they just go home – as many of them would like to do anyway. That's the first thing – we have the strength of those who defend their own children. The other enormous advantage we have is local knowledge – we know the marshes to the east of

63

here. The enemy does not. If we can lure him there, or so many other treacherous places on these islands that they can never know as we know, then we will win and these marshes will glow red with Roman blood…"

A cheer went up and I felt, perhaps for the first time, that if necessary I could lead armies into battle. But I was chastened all too soon.

"I would like to challenge what has been said."

We all turned towards the grizzled old warrior in boiled leather, his face painted blue as our forefathers once did as they went to war.

Fidelma stepped forward and whispered in Togod's ear.

"I recognise Prince Adair of the Trinovantes," said Togod. "I am grateful to you and your people for coming. Please give us the benefit of your wisdom."

The old warrior rose to his full height, which was considerable.

"I have been lectured by young puppies before and I don't enjoy it," he said. I felt myself reddening.

"I would urge this gathering to resist the idea that we can beat the enemy by harrying him, nibbling away at him."

But that was not what I was saying, though I was already committed to the idea.

"No!" said Adair. "There must come a time when we deal the hammer blow and meet Caesar or his successor in open battle. That was how my grandfather fought the first Caesar under your ancestor Cassivelaun, King Togod. That was in the end how we beat them."

"Is that really true?" I asked Fidelma under my breath. The murmuring that followed died down and I rose again.

I felt it was time to be magnanimous.

"I thank Prince Adair and the Trinovantes. I am grateful for your advice as well, and my brother I know would agree with you. There may indeed come such a moment. All I can say is that we agreed at Osen some weeks ago that it will only come, if it comes at all, when the enemy is weak enough that we can with confidence fling him reeling from our shores in one blow."

The old warrior waved a hand. I could not work out whether he did so in acceptance or dismissal.

What I did know was that the tactical debate may have been settled at Osen between the rulers, but it was far from decided by their commanders.

I should say also that this exchange weighed on me for many years. I still have not resolved it in my own mind. I believe I demonstrated in the years to come that you can hold off an enemy or invader, even when he is much stronger than you are, and do so if necessary for many years. The question is whether you still need to seal the deal, so to speak, with a pitched battle to actually get them to leave. I certainly came to believe, perhaps fatally, that Prince Adair was right.

Still that was many years in the future, and – back then – as we woke the morning after our conference, it was to receive a message that the Romans had finally landed.

It came directly to me with a message from the Cantish commander Prince Drustan in the pale light of dawn. The messenger was utterly exhausted and had a wound on his arm by the shoulder that was still undressed. I gathered from him that the Roman force had landed at Ritupia and may have included up to a thousand ships. So the fleet witnessed by Sarah had been just a small part of the main army, which came direct from the Roman barracks on the Rhine.

I also understood that the vanguard of the army was proceeding slowly along the Old Road that they know in Cant as Watling Street. The relief we felt that they had not landed on the north bank of the Thames after all was soon displaced by the news that Prince Drustan's force had been decimated in their attempt to prevent the landing.

**

Much against my better judgement, we crossed the Thames at low tide some miles east of Trinovan, near King's Stone, and took the Old Road westwards in search of the invaders. I was afraid that our army and our precious chariots were dangerously stretched out for what looked like five miles along the way.

"We are dangerously vulnerable," I said to Togod.

"I agree. But there are no Romans here. They can't be yet. We know they are only just marching out of Ritupia docks. We still have a number of rivers to cross yet."

He was right, of course. Though a peculiar cloud seemed to have gathered between us. I could see he was under great strain from his sense of responsibility, but I found it so hard to reach across to him. It hung heavily on me that, for the first time in our lives, I had no idea what was going on in his mind.

It was slow going and muddy, and it was not until we reached the River Med, and the commanders met together and agreed we would make our stand there, that I began to feel a little safer. We chose the western bank and planned to wait until the Romans were part of the way across. There is a ford there but a narrow one and this seemed like a sensible idea. I have to admit that I welcomed it and so did Verkingor, who was now my constant companion. It was an inspired choice of battlefield - for any other enemy than the armed force that we now faced.

The chariots we put on flat ground to our left, in the north, ready to sweep in when we needed them. The Silurians, I took with me on the right flank. Togod and the main army commanders gathered around the path to the ford. We placed the archers along the side of the road, deep in the forest, together with the slingers from the Durnovaria.

"We have not hidden ourselves as we should have done," said Verkingor confidentially.

I knew immediately he was right. Our strategy had not matched the ground we had chosen to fight on. This kind of ground required more than an element of surprise. Our combined army was hardly the biggest Albion had seen but we had already given our strength away by taking the chariots too close to the river. They simply had to have seen us.

Despite these nerves, I remember the surge of excitement I felt when we saw the sun glinting on the helmets of their advance guard in the distance, on the other side of the river. "They must know we are here by now," said Verkingor.

**

I slept that night with the fighters who found themselves under my command, and with my archers, under a bush near the river bank. But I was restless and woke just before the dawn with a stiff neck from the damp, and a sense of foreboding. I walked up and down making sure I was out of sight of the other side. It may have been that taking this precaution meant that I was also unable to see the activity on the opposite bank half a mile upstream. Then all of a sudden, I heard a splash some way downstream.

Fearing the worst, I dashed over and urged my archers awake. Then, increasingly certain and correspondingly prepared to risk breaking cover - and with my heart in my mouth - I ran for Togod's tent, shouting as I went.

Even so, I soon realised I was too late. By the time I had gone back for my sword, which I had lodged with Verkingor for safekeeping as I had walked around the encampment the evening before, there was an orange glow to the north. By then, our various camps were fully awake, alarmed and arming themselves, but the glow in the sky, the smell of burning suggested that the Romans had attacked our chariots. Once my archers had gathered themselves, we began to march rather haphazardly towards the smell, and we began to hear the shouts and the most terrible screams coming from the other side of the hill.

"We are slaughtering them!" said one of my officers. I don't know if he believed it, or whether he was just encouraging the fighters to follow him, but I did not contradict him.

We advanced as quickly as we could. By the time I saw the Silurian druids dashing into the fray ahead of me, it was pretty clear that we had been surprised somehow.

I found my brother at the top of the hill, with the other senior commanders, staring down sadly at the last stand of the charioteers below them - surprised and outclassed. It was a terrible and bloody sight. You could taste the smuts in the air.

"Caradoc!" he shouted. "We need your archers to cover the

road if the main army is to escape. The whole of the Roman army will be crossing in moments. Can you do it?"

I nodded.

"What happened?" I asked Fidelma, next to me.

"It appears that we hadn't expected the Romans to be able to swim and did not post enough sentries…"

"Swim? In full armour?"

"They have trained their tame Celts to do exactly that, it appears."

"Celts! Can you believe it?" shouted Togod,.

You could hear the crackling of flames from what had once been Camelod's proud chariot division, and it was falling like smuts on me as I sought out Verkingor and the troop of archers who I had somehow, so free of merit, come to command.

"We need to take our chance to escape if we are to fight another day," I explained. He nodded. I wondered what he was thinking. As an Atrebatian, he must have been at least in two minds – but still, he had come…

Not long afterwards, we stood ready on the edge of the hill, hidden behind a belt of trees, facing the Romans ranged on either side of the main track. Behind us, the battered remains of our army were making their retreat. As the first Roman vanguard hove into view, I passed the message for my archers to take aim. Should we fire immediately and pick them off as they came - or should we wait until they were flooding in so that our impact could be really felt.

Seeing my indecision, Verkingor said quietly: "I would wait, sir."

I nodded in acknowledgement. I looked behind us to see the last of our stragglers heading away down the road. I knew we could not wait too long either or we should struggle to escape. I made the agreed signal and there was a strange, still moment of buzzing as the arrows sped towards their mark.

More than a dozen Romans fell and there was shouting as their comrades looked desperately around for shelter. Moments later we were firing again.

May God forgive me for the sense of vindication I felt at this moment. That not just had those invaders who had sullied our soil by invading it would not return home, but that in another sense, every death was a small revenge for Imogen.

When I felt sure we had stopped the Roman advance, even briefly, I gave the signal to withdraw and, moments later, we were all running deeper into the woods and away...

"Verkingor," I said, slowly, as we ran. "I think we need to catch up with our army and form the rearguard."

"You are right, sir. I will follow you and we can rejoin the Silurians."

**

The following day, we were helping the army cross the Thames, most of them using the bridge at Trinovan. I had not realised until then just how long it can take to get a not particularly disciplined army of pushing 10,000 across a river crossing. There are so many precautions to be taken. So many arrangements to be made.

It was not until the afternoon, with our rearguard and the majority of the Silurians safely away that Verkingor and I left the bridge, and the road, and went back the way we had come and there, I suppose – with our small group of archers – our long guerrilla war began. It was to become for me a way of life.

I am not saying, of course, that we could ever have attempted to hold the Romans back at that first Med river crossing using these informal tactics. Just that, if it had been me in command – even with my huge inexperience – I would have stuck to guerrilla fighting.

I feel sure we could not then have suffered quite the defeat we had done.

Not long after we saw the enemy again, I killed my first Roman - may God have mercy on me.

We had surrounded part of their advance party and I watched as Verkingor and his archers, and our handful of Silurians, made short work of them. I had no bow and a moment of inattention was all it took to be surprised by a troop of regular soldiers in their strange skirts and metal bands across their shoulders. Within moments, we were fighting for our lives.

It was hardly the first time I had wielded a sword in anger, but it felt more important somehow. I struck the first one with my sword through his stomach, Roman-style I thought as I shoved and heard his death gurgle. Then suddenly, there were three of them at me. I glanced around and couldn't for a moment see my companions.

I summoned up all my strength and hit out, nicking one of them on the arm. Then suddenly, all three fell to the ground at the same time, a British arrow through their necks, and there was Verkingor, sword in hand dashing towards me.

Never in my whole life have I had such a sense of blessed relief. We lived to fight again.

VIII - Betrayal

I knew, as did Togod, that our failure to halt the Roman advance had also meant that they would inevitably now be able to combine their forces with the troops sent via Vectis, as I now understood from my networks, with General Vespasian – and any others who may or may not have been put ashore elsewhere in Cant.

But ironically, that slowed their progress and allowed us the time to regroup and cross back over the Thames. I don't think we even would have reached there if they had wanted to catch us.

Yet all along, it was also a long, slow and tortuous business, a Roman invading army on the move – with its strange baggage train of cooks, prostitutes and engineers, and we harried them all as they struggled along.

I have to say that I felt more alive then than I have done at any other period of my life. I was learning how to fight a superior force, and learning alongside Verkingor in a way that I found inspiring. I could never say that I *enjoyed* it exactly – we lost too many men and women for that. But it was exciting, and I learned my skill at fighting and at command.

The commanders agreed that we should try to lure the Romans across the Thames at Trinovan bridge and into the marshes to the east of the town. I know now that my brother's worries were voluminous, but not least among them had been whether the people of Trinovan would welcome an army led by himself, the son of Cunobelin, who had left the Trinovantes with no hinterland at all, beyond their own big city. Or whether, indeed, they would even allow him to cross the river.

In the event, I understand, he need not have worried. I feel sure the merchants of the town were keen to embrace the Romans, since they already traded with them so successfully. Yet when the mobile rearguard which I commanded reached the bridge some days later, we were welcomed with flowers and gifts by the town's inhabitants.

I led my archers and other irregulars after the main body and we camped in the huge and notorious forest that lies just to the east of Trinovan bridge.

Some of my people were nervous about bedding down in a forest they believed to be haunted, dark and malign. I told them that it would be even more malign for the Romans, then I hurried to find Togod.

I found him sitting alone in the royal tent, the fire from the doorway shining on his forehead. He had his head in his hands and seemed to be shaking.

"Togod," I said. "What, by the old gods, can be the matter?"

"Caradoc. Am I the only one who can see clearly the peril that our nations stand under? You seem to behave as if this was some kind of game."

I confess I hardly knew how to reply. His criticism stung because, on one level, I knew he was right. On the other hand, being the king meant you had to be big enough to see the whole picture and to survive it. One look at my brother convinced me he feared he was not. I decided not to make this kind of criticism.

"Have you not heard the news from the Castle of the Maidens? From the Durotrigians?"

"How could I have? I've been commanding your rearguard for the last couple of weeks."

The Augustan legion under General Vespasian laid siege there after they took the isle of Vectis and have slaughtered every one of the inhabitants for resisting them. If that happens across Britain, who will be responsible? ME! I will!"

"Because you are the King?" I asked gently.

"Yes, because I am the commander in battles. And my name will be execrated for all ages and I will go to hell."

"Surely the Romans will go to hell, not you?"

At this, Togod suddenly leapt to his feet. I could see he had become really angry.

"Don't chop logic with me like a druid. I am the King! I have to take the decisions about what kind lives my people will live – if we can win and if we cannot … out!"

A servant boy had come in with a bottle of red wine – and

72

dashed straight out again.

"What is more," he wasn't shouting now – "our own force has now been depleted because the Durotrigians have gone home and, though I have tried to stop them, we may lose the Dumnonians. Why? Because Vespasian is believed now to be marching north with his Belgian allies. And, in all conscience, I can't prevent them."

"The Dumnonians?" I knew what an important element they made in our own army.

"Right, so now what should we do? Should we fight or come to some kind of terms…?"

Now it was my turn to get angry.

"Oh I see! That's the way your mind is going – well, forget it! The Romans will make no terms now…"

I had bitter cause to remember this conversation when the immediate fighting was over. I also believed passionately in what I said: invaders do not make terms when they are close to success or when they have actually invaded. But once again, the main argument at the council meeting that evening was not whether or not to make terms. It was between the advocates of pitched battle and those, like me, who preferred more subtle methods to wear the enemy down.

"Wear the enemy down!" said Venutis in a not terribly rare moment of ill temper – I could not see how he and Cartimandua were well-matched. "Some of us here want to beat them once and for all, not just *whittle* away at them. Or don't you believe they can be beaten?"

"I refuse to be cast as less confident just because we disagree about tactics," I said.

"Very well," said Togod quietly, almost to himself. "So be it."

He appeared to have come to some kind of conclusion. God help me, at the time I believed he was agreeing with me.

**

As we argued back and forth that night, as it turned out, the first Roman patrols were probing our defences through the marshes. They were mostly as frightened of this damp forest as our people were – my archers reported strange will o' the wisp flames appearing suddenly out of those noxious meres, and the soft screams that we could all of us hear amongst the trees.

Perhaps it was because of this that our defences held except in the centre when a Roman death-or-glory type, who I later discovered was called Hamo, managed to reach a defensible island just behind our lines and, having reached it, could not be dislodged.

I still believe it to have been a discouraged and bedraggled army that faced us outside that forest the next morning. I believed then, and I believe now, that we were ready for them. My archers were on the left this time on dry ground as the first line of defence. Behind us waited the Silurians, and on the right Togod commanded what remained of the Camelod chariots, the sharpened blades on their wheels shining in the pale dawn light.

I could see the banners streaming behind our waiting armies from so many of the various nations of Britain. There was Togod's banner behind his chariot – the red lion and the seven stars – just as I used to see flying behind our father as he hurried into battle. You could see how excited the horses were, and hear the occasional whinny. You could hear the harnesses shaking too, all the way over to where I was standing. And you could feel people's nerves, steeling themselves for the fight of their lives. Now that the sun was emerging, you could catch the occasional glint on a waiting battleaxe or polished shield.

Out of earshot, but still visible through the early morning haze, there was the invading army, disciplined and uniformed in red and bronze – drawn up and waiting patiently for orders. My allotted task was to continue to harry the enemy as they emerged from the woods and the marshes and to make it hard for them to get into any kind of formation. I did this with alacrity, and found I had to restrain them from venturing too close and in the open. We were also being bombarded as soon as they could see us. Arrows were beginning to pour out of the marshes. Togod would have to give some kind of signal pretty soon.

I was mainly safe just inside the forest. On one occasion, I felt it necessary to venture out to urge my archers back under cover. As I fell over the body of a fallen comrade, a Roman arrow through her neck, I saw a raiding party coming fast towards me. In what seemed like an instant, they were on me.

I shouted, got with difficulty to my feet in the damp ground and swung my long sword towards the first of my helmeted attackers. His left arm fell to the grass with a small splash, and he collapsed in a haze of blood and pain. Then the next one came.

Luckily for me, by then Verkingor was again at my side and there was a flurry of arrows and the band of attackers fell dead. We made a hasty retreat back to the trees.

"I think it is time we moved back!" I shouted at Verkingor. He gave the signal and, moments later, we had moved back beside the Silurians on our own front lines.

What I saw there, not long after it became clear that the Romans were attempting to advance, has lived with me ever since.

"Look!" shouted Verkingor, staring at our own lines.

There were our remaining chariots, the Camelod cavalry, with Togod's banner fluttering in the breeze, moving slowly and sedately forward as if leaving the ensuing battle.

"What? What's he doing?" Our lines were silent, watching what was happening.

It was only when the Roman lines opened to admit him and then let out a huge cheer that I began to understand - my own brother had abandoned us and gone over to the enemy.

**

Why did he do it? At the time I simply could not understand but, over the years that have followed, and for various reasons, I have begun to realise a little of why he took that decision. I still don't believe he was right, but – looking back – I know he had tried to explain a little to me as we argued back and forth the evening before. He feared that, unless we came to terms, the Romans would slaughter everyone, destroy the druids and send our wives and our children as slaves across the empire – or worse. He felt, rightly or wrongly, as the heir to Cunobelin, that he was responsible and it was up to him – since it seemed to him that we could not win on the battlefield – to broker some kind of deal.

I also know that, despite his sacrifice, that is virtually what has happened. I find it hard to forgive him even now, since it seems to me that his action made this collapse of the world we knew more likely, not less. I have never met him since so perhaps it no longer matters, but I would like to be reconciled with my brother now he is a client king and I am in exile. I would like to forgive him too, since that is what I have been taught I must do to win eternal life.

But I also knew he had been encouraged in this fantasy by a Roman posing as a go-between, but whose real agenda was entirely destructive. And, since this was the same man who killed my sister, I find it even harder to forgive him.

So, as I stood silently and open-mouthed at my brother's defection, that name kept on going round and round in my head, until I spoke it out loud – "Scapula!" I said.

It was then that I heard my name shouted virtually in my ear and I came to and remembered where I was – standing with our soldiers before a Roman army of invaders, with tears streaming down my face.

"Caradoc! Sir!" Verkingor bawled again. "We must…!"

"I know, I know," I said, aware that our whole host might be looking to me for a lead, now that Togod had gone. What I did now could make the difference between disaster and living to fight another day. I realised now just how many eyes were upon me. It really was up to me.

"Verkingor! Can you get me a horse? A big one?"

I took off my helmet so that I could be seen more easily. Within minutes, I was galloping with him beside me to the front and centre of our line. "To me! To me!" I shouted. "We have the enemy in our trap. Let us now close it… There may come a day when we shall go down to bitter defeat. But that is *not* today – today we are going to fight and to win!"

Starting near me then rolling through our lines, I could hear a cheer - half-hearted at first but then beginning to turn into what I hoped would sound like a roar of defiance.

Yet even as I said it, I doubted whether we could win a pitched battle without our chariots. Worse, I could see our few remaining chariots were already engaged. I could already see that Hamo had taken the opportunity to break out of his defensive lair and was burning the remaining chariots as he went.

"I just don't know," I said to Verkingor. "I'm not sure this can possibly work. Can you take the archers – over to the edge of the forest over there. And be ready to cover our withdrawal – we *will* live to fight another day."

The Roman front line was now advancing, slowly and inexorably. Yet there was Prince Adair withdrawing his troops from the centre. I had to do something. I rode to my Silurians on the right and urged them to fall on the right of the Roman advance, which were peculiarly detached from the centre, partly because of the success of Hamo with the remaining chariots. It was then, I believe – though I did not know it at the time – that an arrow pierced the forehead of my cousin King Guider.

Because I was mounted, I felt I towered above the little Romans and I dashed into the melee, slashing about me. It was when I turned to go back the way I came that I realised how fast the enemy was coming. Not only were the Silurians now in danger because of my brother's defection, but I was now myself in imminent danger of capture.

I urged them back, aware that nobody was following them. In fact, even before meeting the enemy our own lines appeared to have caught infectious panic.

It was time to leave before it was too late. I could see that Verkingor and the archers were now in position, and I swept back up our remaining lines, urging the commanders to withdraw back to Camelod, past the archers.

I have no idea, two whole generations later if I took the right decision that day, and whether we really had any chance of holding Camelod against this all-conquering army. Or whether I made an error the British have been paying for ever since, first in blood and then in slander. Either way, a serious rout was now under way. Across what had once been our chosen battlefield, I could see the eagles advancing. If anyone's blood was flowing, it was ours.

"Come on, it's time to go," I said to my handful of close mounted companions. And we turned our horses away and galloped from the field. It was a shameful end.

VIII - Escape and marriage

For only the fourth time in my life, I stood at the strange overgrown border to the tiny Kingdom by the Sea. The somewhat unkempt and bedraggled gateway on the other side of land owned by no man, beside the great temple of change on Changeburh Hill, had space for a small waiting area.

I have no idea how the wizened, ancient retainer knew that I was there, waiting to be admitted, but she did. By the look of the place, not many passed that way – yet I had seen so many patients on my first visit - but soon I was being conducted inside the strange twisted bramble path, up and up, to the vast, crumbling edifice of Bryn Ciss.

I had had more than enough time to reflect on what had happened during the long and peculiar journey I had made there since I had fled the battlefield of the marshes.

It was a desperate moment in my life and all those I had known and loved. Desperate, I must assume, also for my twin brother Togod, who had cast his lot in with the invaders. You never know what *would* have happened if you had acted differently, and I have no doubt that he was wondering whether – had we stood firm that day – whether we would have won the day and history would have been different.

But I also know that these kind of regrets work both ways. If I had understood better what was on his mind – and how much, even then, he was being influenced by Scapula and his colleagues and supporters in Camelod – perhaps I might have broken the spell, the power they held over him. Equally, perhaps, if we had fought that day and believed in it, maybe even more would have died, and we might still have lost.

As I galloped along towards the great river, filled with regrets, all I knew for certain was that I must be avenged on that Roman somehow, sometime – and not now just for the death of my sister, but also the defection and perversion of my brother.

When we felt safe enough to stop, I asked my colleagues to

go their separate ways, and I sent via one of them a message to my cousin Arvir in Siluria, partly about his brother's death which I now knew about, and agreed to meet him there if I possibly could - and to spread the word to any surviving stragglers from our army to do the same. There would be no time for me to make sure I would be named king in succession to Togod. But what could I do – the Romans would be at the gates of Camelod before I could?

I asked Verkingor if he would ride fast to Cameold and get my sister Gwladys out before the Romans arrived. He agreed and I am not ashamed to say that there were tears rolling down my cheeks as I watched him mount his horse and to go.

I crossed the Thames west of Trinovan at the King's Stone, disguising myself as a merchant, and headed south - aware that the great southern forest may be my best hiding place. And if I was nervous about crossing it, I could be pretty sure my pursuers would also be.

It was near the King's Stone that I heard the news about the submission of the Durotrigians to Vespasian. That meant the Romans had divided the country into two, down a neat line between Trinovan and the western channel – potentially dividing me from the Silures. I was unsure, I confess, of the best way to go to guarantee my arrival with Arvir.

It was some miles past there, with Trinovan in sight, beside the ancient Island of Thorns, that I encountered what turned out to be the vanguard of General Vespasian's army, seeking to link up with the main body. It nearly put an end to my resistance campaign before it had even begun.

I think my mistake was to reply to them in Latin when they asked who I was. "My name is Seisil the merchant," I said, "from Trinovan. I trade in wine along the coast."

They were immediately suspicious, aware how few of those of us who live in these islands can speak Latin. Yet also unaware of how many merchants can and do – I had been too clever for the Roman military that time, and for myself as well.

"OK, come with us," said the centurion. "We have orders to take anyone of fighting age to be questioned by my master."

I entreated, of course. I explained that my ship was waiting to sail from the strand in Trinovan, but it was to no avail. So soon, I was being marched in manacles along with five other men from various tribes, mainly I would say Atrebatian, plus one Belgian. We made slow shuffling progress in the sunshine along the road parallel to the river on the south side, towards the gates of Trinovan itself.

I noticed that Vespasian's army did not follow us, but went straight across the river at the low sandy crossing place by the Island of Thorns. I expect he was in a hurry to reach the main army, which I now understood was under the command of a relative of the Emperor called Aulus Plautius.

Where the road turned left to Trinovan bridge, there was an old inn called the Tabard, outside which our guard was relieved, and our manacles removed because they needed them back. I was exhausted and thirsty and did not relish the prospect of questioning by Roman officers.

I was just wondering how I could contrive some kind of escape when, suddenly, an extraordinary sound like trumpets sounded ahead of us along the Old Road. Then, what should turn the corner, with a powerful force behind them, but two grey monsters with the most enormous white tusks, tramping down the dust along the road to Trinovan. They looked something out of a druidic beastiary, and because of my long training I knew that these were elephants – probably elephants of war – which could only mean one thing: the Emperor himself could not be far behind.

Now I understood exactly how and why the Roman commander Plautius had made such slow progress since the battle of the marshes – by accounts, he had barely moved from the battlefield. It had nothing to do with waiting for Vespasian. He was waiting for the Emperor to arrive himself to claim 'his' victory – presumably from the very throne in Camelod that I should perhaps have been occupying myself, in the absence of Togod.

We, all of us, Briton and Roman alike, stared at the elephants as they swayed towards us. They had not got around to replacing my manacles, so – as the elephants came closer –

I realised this was an opportunity if I acted quickly.

The attention of the soldier guarding me was as much taken with the monsters as everyone else's. I whispered to him: "Legionary!" Then, as he turned towards me to hear better against the noise of the beasts, I kneed him hard in the balls and – in a quick movement, once he had doubled up in pain – I grabbed his sword and drew it quickly from his scabbard.

Before his fellows noticed what was happening, I had him in a grip with the sword at his throat. "Quick," I hissed. "Unshackle my friends."

The other Britons captured with me began to catch on and put out their manacled hands. One by one and achingly slowly, the Roman gestured to his colleague to do so.

"And any noise by either of you, and this man loses his windpipe," I warned. "Now, stand still while we borrow your swords…"

In the dust thrown up by the elephants, it was still extraordinary that none of the other soldiers appeared to have noticed what was happening.

"Who is your master?" I whispered in the ear of the soldier with whom I had the intimacy with of holding a knife to his throat. "Who commands you?"

"We are an independent unit," he said, rather apologetically. "Our task is to seek out possible spies. We report to Julius Ostorius Scapula."

Of course they did, I thought to myself. Scapula and me seemed bound together by fate.

"Well, give your friend Scapula a message from me, Seisil the Merchant. We Britons will never be slaves. Yours or anyone else's."

Then I shouted to my colleagues in the hope that they would follow.

"Come on, into the woods!"

I ran in that direction myself, hoping that the sounds of running behind me came from British and not Roman feet.

The woods were behind a small village of huts that marked the spot where the Old Road turned in towards Trinovan. If we could make it there, I hoped we could find the horses we needed to escape.

Sure enough, the five of us fell panting at the cattle trough in the village, and there were indeed horses tethered there.

"But they are not ours," complained my companion from Trinovan.

Typical, I thought. What is it about the Trinovantes that makes them obsessed with who owns what?

"Needs must," I said. Two of us got on the first horse and we were off and away towards the woods by the time the Romans had got themselves together to start any kind of pursuit.

**

The arrogance of the Cants and the people of the South Country really takes the breath away. When were safely away, I began to ask the direction from my companions – I felt it best not to reveal who I was – but they had never heard of the great southern forest. They said I was on the edges of something called the Great North Wood. As if everything important has to be called for them alone. North Wood, I ask you! North of where exactly? The sea?

Still, we thanked each other and went on our way once we had reached the first ridge, from where you can look down towards Trinovan and the river. They pointed me in the direction of the next ridge, from the top of which I was told you could see Changeburh Hill. I guided my stolen horse down the track through the forest – which I now knew stretched as far as the eye could see in every direction except the one I had left behind.

I had always understood that unwary travellers through this forest will never find the way unless they can find a witch guide. This was no doubt a story put around by the guides themselves – but, equally, I did not want to run the risk of going round in circles until I had died of thirst, so I looked out for one.

But as I approached a gap in the forest, a village I believe was called Capel, I ran into someone better.

"Fidelma! How did you get here?"

Apparently both relieved and afraid to have found me, she disconcertingly fell to her knees.

"Oh come on, Fidelma. I can't have my own tutor kneeling to me!" I said.

"Please forgive me, Caradoc. You can imagine what I advised your brother, but I would not leave him…"

"Of course not; I would expect nothing else," I said, raising her up.

"You do not blame me, then?"

"No, I blame another. One called Scapula."

The look of relief in my old tutor's face almost brought tears to my eyes.

"So why are you here now?"

"Your brother sent me to you. To try to explain, he said."

I was amazed. "Then your divinatory powers are extraordinary. How did you know I would be here?"

She grinned conspiratorially at me.

"I have to be honest. I was heading south to find you at Bryn Ciss. It so happens we chose to go the same way."

"And are you also pursued by the Roman army?" I asked her.

"Well, I…" she said.

We embraced. I had never known Fidelma lost for words before.

"I am glad you knew me well enough to know where I would go."

"Well, Caradoc. The stars and my intuition and knowledge led me here. I knew where you would go even if you did not. But, you forget - I am also skilled in the druidic arts of searching. This was not the coincidence it seems."

"And you knew I would try to reach Siluria by sea? You are clever and your learning is very much deeper than mine."

Fidelma laughed.

"Yes, but you have forgotten to mention one other element in your decisions – a certain princess of the Kingdom by the Sea. You see, I am not entirely uninformed…"

I stared at her open-mouthed.

"You are extraordinary. Now, do your skills extend to

navigating our way through this forest?"

"It isn't hard. Just do as I say and stick to the path," said Fidelma. "And on the way, I will tell you of your brother."

**

A day or so later, exhausted and thirsty and a little drunken with the darkness of the forest path we were venturing down, I thought I heard the sound of a bell.

"Did I hear that, or am I imagining it?" I asked.

This was obviously a surprise for Fidelma, who had clearly heard nothing.

"A bell? Where? Can you walk us towards it?"

Still unsure of this bell actually existed, we struggled on towards the direction it seemed to come from. Fidelma explained to me that there was a famous old crone who lived in a boggy patch near here, and who would tell us what we needed to know. She had hoped to find her here – but she still couldn't hear the bell.

The odd thing was that the closer we came to the bell, the quieter it sounded – as if it reached into the forest to draw us in. Finally the tolling stopped entirely.

"It's stopped. Right, we must have reached the Gate," said Fidelma. "Then we must look around."

And as she spoke, it became clear that we stood beside a kind of opening in the hillock, the rudest possible home and an ancient woman in the dirtiest rags you have ever seen, cross-legged beside it.

Fidelma knelt before her. Then she beckoned me over.

"Do we really want to know?" I whispered frantically as she led me over: if my future was as I feared at that time, I felt I would far prefer not to know about it.

It was too late.

"Approach me, Caradoc of Camelod," said the old woman. This was quickly becoming one of the most terrifying experiences I had ever encountered.

Suddenly there seemed to be many women, all offering me cups of the most foul-tasting liquid. Once I had tasted it, I slept as one dead.

I dreamed first that the old woman was becoming younger and more beguiling and that she offered me herself - and that I refused her, unsure whether this was either safe or the right thing to do. To this day, I still have no idea.

Then the dreams and the hallucinations began…

**

I'm not sure how long after these events it was, but Fidelma and I stood by the gates of Bryn Ciss, which looked even more overgrown and abandoned than it had beforehand.

Yet there – as if they were some kind of divinatory watcher - was Oonag, their old retainer, waiting for us. She took us through up the old path that wound upwards – where once the warriors had come to watch and guard over our island – up until it opened out into the great hall that I remembered from my previous visit.

The smell of herbs was as strong as before and it added to my dreaminess that had afflicted me since the gate to the River Arun which we had sped down by boat towards the sea, put ashore once again at Old Stone, from whence we took the road to Changeburh by foot.

For a long time in the boat, with just Fidelma and the ferryman, the motion made me believe I had still been inside the trance induced by the crone. Fidelma refused to hear what I had seen, afraid that she had not been allowed to see it by whatever sent it. I have told nobody, not even my family, yet there is no reason why I should not tell now that I am old.

The truth is that I don't really know what I saw, except that I saw myself in Rome again, with the Emperor. I saw myself also with a man I knew to be holy – and a woman too – perhaps holier than anybody else in history. I saw myself discussed by scholars over centuries, but all of them speaking Latin.

Yes, I heard them too - perhaps overheard would be a better description. I saw their history books were all Roman and their stories too. I tried to shout out to them, to tell them that they had got it wrong. I wanted to tell them – how did I know this? – that a Briton would be Roman emperor one day; we came from a magical land, with a special place in history of world, and we should not forget it. We must have pride in our ways. But I knew that we would not.

I was not sad for myself, you understand. I was sad for our history, great as it was, that would be led by Romanised men and women with no memory or understanding of what I feared we were about to lose.

"By the ancient gods," I said to Fidelma. "What possessed you to put me through that ordeal? I have dreamed of the distant future – so far away that I can barely understand it."

"As I have said, Caradoc – you must tell me nothing of it."

What brought me to myself again in that great hall was Sarah, smiling at me, and her dark hair glinting in the light from above. She ran to me and leapt into my arms.

"Caradoc, thank Christ! I have prayed to the lord so much to protect you that I nearly wore my hands out – and he has!"

I kissed her and then I remembered Fidelma. She was watching with a look of amusement on her face.

"Sarah, this is my companion Fidelma…"

"Your companion! This is the great Fidelma who tutored you and taught you? I am so pleased to meet you. You are both so welcome. Come now – my father awaits you."

We went through the long low-ceilinged rooms of patients, some of them sleeping, some of them standing in the doorways to the gardens, through to the ancient throne room.

And there was the King. He looked exhausted but quite calm, so unlike my own father who so rarely looked either. It was one of those moments of indecision and excitement that come along all too rarely. Should I ask for his daughter's hand in marriage, knowing that there would be an untruth at the heart of the request – I would have married her anyway? Or should I simply tell him?

I asked. It seemed the most polite thing to do.

He took my hand and rose to his feet a little unsteadily, with tears in his eyes. "Prince Caradoc," he said. "I would not have parted with her for anyone but you – yet you know that a perilous road lies ahead of you and she will have to share that peril. I have prayed long and hard to know the best course for her, and I believe the bold approach may be the safest for her to take as well. So I give my consent willingly."

If this was a romance, sung by a druid, then the last act would follow when I had asked Sarah to marry me. But it is not romance; this is history. Even so, we fell into each other's arms and laughed for no obvious reason.

"Where is Fidelma?" I asked, aware that I had not seen her for some time.

"She is at the lookout post – Oonag is showing her." I remembered the extraordinary position, high in the downs, from where you could see far out across the ocean in every direction. It had been the main function of the palace of Bryn Ciss before Sarah and her father brought in their herbs and healing.

"There is a problem about getting married," said Sarah. "I follow the Way – the Way, the Truth and the Light – and there are no priests able to marry within hundreds of miles. I believe we may have to take matters into our own hands."

I was unsure what she meant. But she took me by the hand and led me out of the palace and down the slope above the sea to a secluded glade.

"We can marry here," she said. "Now."

To emphasise this, she kissed me full on the lips. And we lay next to each other and I removed her clothes and then my own, and we loved each other as she smiled up at me.

It was the most wonderful afternoon of love, and I look back on it now, as an old man, as if it justifies everything else I ever did.

"One thing worries me," I said, as I held her there in my arms under the sun. "I thought you Hebrews believed that we had to be married to do this?"

"Oh, I don't know," she said thoughtfully. "God sees all. He knows we love each other and he believes in love. And although I'm a Hebrew by race, I am only a Hebrew by religion in so far as I am a follower of Christ and Christ came to *fulfil* the law. The stories show that he didn't believe in sticking too closely to the letter of the rules.

"He didn't believe in pettyfogging rules?"

"No, I think he would understand that we are now man and wife in his sight."

"I like that," I said. "I believe that."

"Especially when the nearest priest is in Siluria…"

"In Siluria! But that is where I have to go next! If we are now man and wife, then why don't we go together?"

"Caradoc," she said simply. "I will."

IX - The Isle of Apples

If General Vespasian had driven a military wedge across
Albion between west and east, it made getting to Siluria
difficult indeed. What were we to do? With Fidelmas's help,
we decided that I would continue my disguise as Seisel the
Merchant, and take a ship from the wharf at Old Stone along
the coast to the West. There were sailings most days, then and
now, as there always had been.

It took some days for Sarah to hand over responsibilities for
her patients to Fidelma who opted to stay, and to gather her
possessions and say farewell to her father and friends. She
spent much of the time in tears and I felt a deeply guilty. Many
times, I offered to go alone, but each time she kissed me
lightly and carried on with her preparations.

I said farewell to Fidelma, unsure whether we would ever
meet again. Old Stone was only an hour or so to walk to from
Bryn Ciss and it took little time to negotiate a price with the
master of one of the ships to take us as far as Dumnonia, from
where the plan was to find another boat to go beyond.

Sarah wept copiously as we left, but we grew together as we
lay off unfamiliar harbours every night, wrapped in skins,
watching the stars above us – or kept watch for the temples
along the way which had lit fires nightly to prevent unwary
seamen falling upon the rocks.

On the way, I told her stories of life at Camelod under
Cunobelin, of the three-storey palace and the wine and the
olives. And she told me stories of the Way – of Jesus of
Nazareth, who was the son of God long foretold by the
Hebrew's holy texts, put to death under the Romans, and how
– three days later – he had risen again. And how many of his
followers had accompanied his great uncle Joseph to Siluria to
escape persecution by the authorities.

I have no idea what she made of my stories, but hers kept me
on the edge of my wooden seat. Towards the end of our first
day at sea, with the Isle of Vectis visible ahead, I stared

towards the harbour at Wood Town near New Fields, imagining that I could catch a glimpse of Togod, where I believe he had been installed already as some kind of client king.

It was not difficult in Dumnonia to find a second captain who would take us around the tip of these islands and later into the strange murky inlets of southern Siluria, where the very homes and villages are built on water.

I needed to find my cousin King Arvir, who now ruled these strange watery people. But, although, we asked wherever we ventured, few seemed to have heard of kings, let alone where we might find this one. Luckily, Sarah was much more specific. She knew where we were going almost by instinct, though she had not been before, or so she claimed. She asked for a strange place she called the Isle of Apples.

Finally, we found a captain who knew where she meant, though he told us that navigation could be difficult in the autumn. And so it was that we stepped ashore at a remote dock – barely a landing stage – beyond the marshes of Siluria called All Weary Hill. We clambered out with our few possessions. There was nobody here to meet us – how could there have been and there was little chance we would encounter our invaders in this distant and inaccessible spot.

We walked down the difficult path through the mist and the land felt even wetter the further we went. At length, there appeared a peculiar hill, in the shape of a breast, rising out of the mist ahead of us. On the first risings of this hill, the path took us to a gateway, where we knocked and were eventually admitted.

"May I ask your name?" A young man with an unusual accent met us and led us inside.

I felt irritable and difficult.

"I am Caradoc, High King of the British races by right of my father Cunobelin, and this is my wife Sarah. We ask for sanctuary."

This did not seem to surprise him, until I mentioned Sarah's name, which he appeared to recognise.

He bowed politely and beckoned us forward. We could see a

number of rude huts stretching into the distance and one large building of mud and clay, still unfinished. The man preceded us into the second hut and we followed him in.

An old man sat there who now rose with difficulty to greet us.

"My name is Joseph," he said. "May God's blessings be upon you. How can I help you?"

Rather disconcertingly, Sarah fell immediately to her knees.

"Please get up, my dear," said the old man. "There is no reason to bow to me."

"We are looking for King Arvir," I said. "I seek sanctuary with my cousin."

"Then please, sit down with me," he said. "You must be tired and hungry after your journey. I will get you some refreshment. I am a mere trader in tin; I am not one of the great ones of faith."

"You are Joseph of Arimathea," I said, bowing. "My wife has told me about you. She is a follower of the Way."

"And you are not, my son?"

"Well, to be honest, I know too little to know. I have lost my father's city to the Romans, lost my brother to them too. I lost my beloved sister to a Roman monster and feel I almost have nothing left to lose – except for Sarah who you see before you here. I am making my way to my cousin King Arvir to see what, between us, we might save.'

The old man thought hard before replying.

"Of course, I understand. I have heard about you from Arvir, who discussed you many times. When you have rested and recovered here, he has asked me when you arrive - to send you to him at Caer Leon. You must know that Arvir has been good to us. He gave us the land we live on here. I baptised him myself…"

"You baptised him?" I said, unsure what that implied.
Joseph laughed.

"Don't look so alarmed. Has Sarah not explained to you what how we make followers in the Way of Christ? It just requires a little water and there is no shortage of that here."

"We want you to marry us!" Sarah blurted out.

"Aha, well then I fear there is a problem. For marriage requires priests and, when your movement believes Christ is due again to turn the world upside down, then there is little time to work out how to create them. For my part, I believe the world is likely to last rather longer yet than I once felt in Palestine. We argue among ourselves about it. But I don't know, and neither do any of us, what our lord actually thought himself. Sometimes he spoke as if the world was on the very brink. Sometimes he spoke as if the decisions and revolutions were things that must happen first in our own hearts. Oh, yes, but we have had some marriages in the Way over the last few years. I am a rabbi, so yes I would be delighted to marry you. But first, you rest. It may not be dry here, but it is at least warm…"

**

"Who did you say you wanted us to meet?" I asked Joseph that evening, when the light began to dim and he took us around some of the other huts.

"Just here," he said simply. "I know she would like to meet you."

He led me to the door of a hut on the edge of their encampment. The sun was streaming still on the conical hill above us.

"You did know, didn't you, that among the companions when we made our escape from Palestine to Massalia a couple of years ago, was Jesus's mother?"

Before I had time to reply, we were inside. There was a strong brazier when we arrived. It struck me how cold these damp Silurian evenings must seem to people brought up in the heat of the Mediterranean – especially if they were getting on in years.

As it was, the lady who greeted us must have been fifty or sixty winters old, yet perhaps it was her obvious wisdom and her experience of exile – from family and loved ones too – that made her seem older. Yet there was a glimmer of amusement in her eyes which made her feel younger too. We fell to our knees before her.

"No, no, come come," she said, through Joseph who translated for us. "I will not have the High King and Queen of Britain bow to me!"

I did not know what to say and clearly she did not need words.

"In that case, perhaps I should welcome you on behalf of the people of our island nations," I said. "But I am only High King by default, because my brother has gone over to the Romans. I haven't even been crowned."

"You do understand why the Romans are here, don't you?" said Joseph, taking care to translate what he said for Mary.

"You mean, did they really come to put King Verica back on the throne of Atrebatia? No, I don't think so either."

"Nor for the tin. Or for the silver, come to that."

"Why then, do you believe?"

"I am afraid they are here for us. We have brought this disaster on you. They know what the Way means for their pagan ways, their Mithras and their emperor worship. They didn't mind when we were a small Jewish sect in Palestine, but only ten years now since our Lord rose from the dead and we are already almost round the whole world. Even in Rome."

"And you believe they are here to capture you? Are you worried?"

"Oh no, I don't think they are interested in finding us, though – if they did – they will have trouble finding us here. They don't want Britain to become the heart of a religion that will in the end spread across the world. They need to be here to make sure that doesn't happen."

I was a little sceptical of this interpretation.

"You don't think that the vanity of a new emperor is enough explanation?"

"There are so many other places, easier places to invade, if that was all it was," said Joseph. "They want to nip us in the bud, I fear. Whether you are baptised or not, Caradoc, or one of us or not – you are defenders of the true faith against the barbarians. You all believe in God, do you not?"

We talked a little, me and Sarah and the mother of God, and

then Sarah dared one more question. It is one I knew she wanted the answer to.

"May I ask you a difficult and personal question?" she asked.

Mary looked at Joseph as he translated, then she smiled and nodded.

"You gave birth to Jesus. You brought him up through his childhood. Can you really believe he was part of God too?"

She laughed a little when she heard the question.

"She is laughing because that is such a typical question for this country," said Joseph with a smile. "I don't know why."

She held Sarah's hand as she answered.

"Yes, you are right. I looked at him as any mother looks after their child, so I'm afraid I don't know the answer to your question," she said. "There are cleverer people than I who understand such things better. But I do know this – that he rose from the dead and some things are only possible for God. So maybe he was and maybe he wasn't. But for God, all things are possible. Do you understand?"

I nodded and found myself inexplicably in tears, as I saw Sarah was too. It was moving to see this small woman, who had endured so much and lost so much, eking out her remaining days in the cold and damp of southern Siluria, speaking with such warmth and animation about such mysteries.

Outside, I asked Joseph if he would also baptise me into the Way.

**

"I had not told you before," said Joseph, as he and a number of others accompanied Sarah and myself down to a spring below the hill. "But King Arvir sent a ship for you that arrived some days ago."

"How did he know we were coming this way?"

"I don't know if he did. I believe he sent ships to various other places too."

I realised this was also the way that Joseph could say

goodbye. He was explaining that the water of life would take us, one way or the other.

I remember little about the baptism, just the cold of the water when Joseph of Arimathea held me there in the marshes and I accepted Jesus as my Lord and promised to follow him.

Afterwards, shivering by the fire in the entranceway, I wondered whether I had been right to take such vows when I had also accepted another task.

"Joseph, I feel bad that I still find it so hard to forgive."

"Baptism does not make you suddenly perfect, Caradoc," he said. "It provides you with a way to go further, a direction to take – that is all. Who can you not forgive - can you tell me?"

"My brother and the Roman who killed my sister."

"Your brother Togod?"

"Now he calls himself Togidumnus. He has Romanised himself, and he has proclaimed himself king in the south…"

"You have told me much of him already and his reasons for changing sides, and his pain. I believe you understand him and have already forgiven him. The Roman is harder, I see that. We just have to pray about those things we just cannot achieve by ourselves. Only Jesus can do it and he can help us. That is what I believe - and he has helped. Believe me, Carodoc – I have lost such friends and loved ones already, and by deliberate decision of those who hate us. I know how hard it can be to forgive."

I shivered some more and drew closer to the fire. I wished Fidelma were here.

"There is another more difficult matter too. You know why I am going north tomorrow? I am planning to lead the resistance to the Romans. I am no man of peace. You know that, don't you?"

Joseph was silent for a while and stared into the fire beside me.

"I do know that, of course. And I sin perhaps myself too in wanting you to win, but we have to give up such affections. God will decide one way or the other, whether we face a better future ourselves before the Way wins out and what bloodshed we will have to face before that happens."

He was breathing hard now.

"I believe that to take someone's life always it is against the will of God. We have not discussed these things as a Church yet, though perhaps we will be able to one day. But I think there may be a way that God sees the self-sacrifice of a man or woman who risks everything to defend their neighbour. Wouldn't you? We are imperfect people and we must pray to become less so – always aware that we can't do it by ourselves. Only God can do that."

Joseph rose and embraced us both.

"God be with you, Sarah and Caradoc. I will pray for you to find the right path."

**

And so we were married again the following day, and we took our vows to each other in the old druid way and using Jewish and Christian lines, and they all sounded remarkably the same. We stood next to each together in the sweltering, misty heat from the fires in their half-built mud church. We were crowded inside: I could see Mary at the back and some of Jesus's companions. Outside, I could see the mists gathering too, arising up from the marshes.

"I don't believe anybody has been as married as we are," I told Sarah quietly. "Three times – three sets of vows! Can you believe it?"

"*Four* times," she whispered. "Don't forget we also married ourselves with a different kind of vow altogether."

We held each other's hands. I was bowled over by how brave she was to ally herself to me at the moment in history, when I was a wanted man across a whole empire – the one which I feared we had just been annexed into.

I was aware also that if they knew both Arvir and I had been baptised into the Way, we would prove such a challenge to the empire that they would not rest until they had rooted us out.

And yet I also felt a great calm, knowing that whatever was to happen to us would be right, that we were in God's hands and that my whole life had been in preparation for this moment.

Then we gathered our meagre belongings and walked down the wharf on All-Weary Hill to meet the captain sent by Arvir to take us north to the city of Caer Leon. I looked back at the gentle Silurian hills in the evening light and knew then that everything had shifted. Then, hand in hands with Sarah, we turned to face the uncertain sea.

Endnote

Caractacus must have written his biography in exile in Rome, assuming he wrote one, but no copy of it has survived. So unfortunately, there was no translator involved here. I was first alerted to his extraordinary story in Graham Robb's brilliant book *The Ancient Paths,* one of a growing number of historians and writers to start rethinking our pre-Roman past. But it was George Jowett's strange and peculiar book *The Drama of the Lost Disciples* which got me thinking about Caractacus for the first time.

Jowett died in 1969 after a distinguished career as a boxer, publisher and planner in Canada. But the research behind the book, in the Vatican archives, is an equally important legacy. His argument was that, according to the archives, it wasn't just Joseph of Arimathea who came to Britain in 38AD, as legend suggests – it was the Virgin Mary and many of the surviving disciples of Jesus who took refuge in Glastonbury that year, joined later by St Peter and St Paul. Jowett's plea was that, given that the medieval church recognised this claim by giving British bishops precedence at the great councils of the Church – we ought to take this more seriously. Or at least as seriously as the flawed and compromised memories of Roman writers with axes to grind.

If this was right, Jowett suggested, then it may provide a different interpretation to the Roman invasion five years later. It may also be that Caractacus, as the archives suggest, was not a backward pagan type, but Christian king battling the pagan Romans and desperately trying to hold back their tide of brutality.

I have written Caractacus' autobiography as if Jowett was right. As such, I am attempting to strike a small blow against a those generations of positivist scholars who identified with the Romans more than with their forebears defending our homeland – who regarded the invaders as 'we', and continue to try to subdue the real spirit of these islands ever since.

Caractacus managed to stand alone for nearly nine years against the biggest and most sophisticated army in the known world. Why did he? Because he was a civilised, intelligent man fighting the crass brutality of the Romans.

As such, we have had to rediscover the original names of people and places from the Roman documents which – just as one might expect from Italians to this day – tended to add a couple of syllables. So we have Togod not Togodubnus and Caradoc not Caractacus, or their father Cunobelin not Cunobelinus. We have also had to update the traditional Roman names for the so-called 'tribes' of Britain, aware that these were not so much tribes as separate and civilised nations. Hence Atrebatia, Brigantia, Siluria and Cant.

That may make it more difficult to interpret the place names, especially Trinovan, a shortening of the pre-Roman name for London, Trinovantum (at least according to Geoffrey of Monmouth). Some other place names, in case this is helpful. See also the map on www.david-boyle.co.uk/caractacus

Brigantia Yorkshire and Northumberland
Caer LeonCaerleon
CallevaSilchester
Camelod Colchester (Latin: Camelodunum)
CantKent (as in Canterbury)
Castle of MaidensMaiden Castle, Dorset
ChangeburhChanctonbury Ring, Sussex
CissCissbury Ring, Sussex
Dumnonia West Country (Cornwall and Devon)
DurnovariaDorchester
DurotrigiaDorset
Gate Slinfold (means 'gate' in old Sussex dialect)
HomeHampstead
IceniaEast Anglia (Norfolk and Sussex)
Isle of ApplesGlastonbury (said to be the meaning of the word 'Avalon')
King's StoneKingston, Surrey
New FieldsChichester
Old StoneSteyning, Sussex

OsenOsney, Oxford (Graham Robb says this was considered to be the geographical centre of Britain)
OsenfordOxford
RitupiaRichborough, Kent
SiluriaGwent, Somerset and Gloucestershire
TrinovanLondon
Vectis Isle of Wight
Venta BelgaeWinchester
Wood TownBosham, Sussex

Extract from *Regicide* by David Boyle

**Regicide:
Peter Abelard and the Great Jewel**

David Boyle

Prologue

The New Forest, 2 August 1100

It was one of those long, lazy summer's evenings in southern England, with the dry undergrowth rasping together in a haze of crickets and pollen. The shadows were lengthening, but the sun was still high and the forest glowed with the heavy heat of a waning afternoon. The trees were only one generation old then.

In the murky shadows of the woods were watchers. Some remembered this wooded track when it snaked between villages, hovels and farms, but those places had disappeared in the fifty years since the Norman invaders had imposed their ferocious Forest Laws. It was forbidden to hunt here now, and those caught lost their hands or even their lives, which would be forfeited in the slow, agonising ways favoured by the Normans for their Saxon victims. The forest teemed with game, but families around it had to starve before they could take so much as a rabbit.

That was why the woods were now left empty and echoing, with only the odd mound of stones to remind anybody that this was once a thriving community.

Occasionally the pounding of thundering hooves rang out, with the jingling of spurs, the baying of hounds, and the sound of the horn, but hunting was the preserve of those with the privileges of rank and wealth: the knights and barons who served the king, the churchmen not too fat to mount a horse, and, of course, the king himself.

There were people, though, brave enough to disobey the law and enter the forbidden territory. With their forest skills, they knew how to leave no trail, how to move silently through the undergrowth and how to melt away into the green darkness. Also perhaps a favoured few, licensed to live and ply their trade in the forest, blackened creatures of the woods, the rank smell of charcoal on their clothes who lived off the forest and its fruits.

Today the king was coming to hunt, as he did when in residence at Castle Malwood on the edge of the forest. The day was drawing to a close. He would be here soon. The watchers in the woods were invisible in the shadows, waiting, and one man in blackened leather jacket, his face tar-black from smoke, leaned in the shadows against his charcoal cart.

The sounds of the approach came first – the tramping through the bracken, the slashing of foliage – then the beaters and servants appeared, silent but breathing hard, their eyes focused on the undergrowth, intent on reading the signs there that the quarry might have passed by. In their muddy jerkins and old leathers, they were dressed in the colours of the forest, dull and drab in comparison to the small group who followed behind.

French voices were heard declaiming loudly, and then the Norman lords came sauntering into sight, a vision of bright colour and sumptuous fabrics, glinting with gold and jewels, looking like curious fantastical birds against the murky undergrowth. Their horses, magnificent beasts which probably saw more oats in one evening than a Saxon family did in a month, were held back by the grooms as the lords dispersed into small groups for the ritual business of seeking out the elusive stag. This part of the hunt would be undertaken on foot.

From the general crowd, one man emerged. He was as richly dressed as the others but by his confidence and swagger it was evident that this was the King, the son of the Conqueror himself. He was short, red-haired and pot-bellied, and a little pale, as if he had recently been ill and come out hunting for reasons other than strict enjoyment. He held himself apart from those around him, and issued orders in a rough, barking Norman tongue, sending the groups of lords off in different directions with a flourish of his hand. The noblemen obeyed him without question, and within moments the king was left alone with his hunting partner, a man whose ease with the handling of his bow showed him to be a practiced marksman. The grooms hung back with the horses, waiting until their masters should deign to return.

The king turned to his partner and spoke in a low voice, indicating with a gesture of his hand where he thought they should begin their stalking. The other man nodded, pulling an arrow from his quiver in readiness. The king barked another order and a groom brought forward two horses. The marksman took their reins and the two men set off through the undergrowth together.

Within a few minutes, they approached a clearing, as silent and deserted as the rest of the wood. A light breeze ruffled through the branches, shafts of golden evening sunlight fell through the forest canopy in places, and all was quiet. The two men had a quick muttered conversation, then the marksman looped the horses' reins over a tree branch to tether the beasts while the men walked on into the clearing, where they trod with more care. Beyond the line of trees was, at last, some wetness, and they stepped delicately across the marshy ground. The sun was beginning to dip below the tops of the trees and the first hint of evening chill came from the shadows. The king took up his bow in readiness as he stared into the dimness on the other side of the clearing, and pulled out an arrow. Beyond him, on the edge of the trees, the marksman played his fingers over the string of his bow, already taut in case they should spy their quarry. They were evidently of the mind that the stag was close by now, and did not speak. The king stepped silently into the clearing, out of the boggy ground ready for whatever might emerge from the trees.

Suddenly, there was a rustle in the undergrowth and the sound of cracking wood. The two men swung round separately, the king fumbling his arrow onto the string, the marksman pulling back his elbow and dropping into stance as the stag suddenly burst from the cover behind and skittered between them. The marksman followed its path with his body and let fly his arrow. The string twanged and the arrow hummed through the air. Startled birds fluttered up into the sky in panic, chirruping and beating their wings.

The stag raced free into the undergrowth. A loud, human groan echoed out in the evening air. The king staggered forward, dropping his bow as he clawed desperately at an arrow lodged into his chest. He broke it off as he fell to the ground, first to his knees and then forward, onto the dusty ground, crashing down onto his front, his face buried in the dust. His laboured breathing stopped and there was an eerie silence.

The marksman stared in horror, then ran to the prone body of the king. He spoke rapidly in French, breathless with appalled disbelief. Could the arrow that had struck the king really been his own? He stared at it, too terrified to touch it, unsure whether this was the very shaft that he had been handed earlier. Then the panic came. Sheer terror possessed him and he began to shake, his face dead white. In the distance were the voices of the other Norman lords. They were approaching, no doubt led to the spot by the appearance of the fluttering birds. As his nerve deserted him utterly, the marksman dropped his bow, slipped off his quiver, turned his back on the dead man and ran across the clearing to where the horses waited in the undergrowth. There was his mount. He took the reins, hauled himself onto its back and turned its head away from the clearing, and in the opposite direction to the approaching voices. He kicked his heels to its flanks, and urged it off at speed.

In the dark shadows, the watchers began to melt away. They must leave before it became known that they had witnessed this dark corner of history. One darted forward towards the clearing and from the leafy ferns, broken by the stag's flight, he scrabbled for a moment before lifting out an arrow, then hurried back to join the others as they fell back into the depths of the forest. The man with the blackened face moved carefully back into the shadows. They were invisible when the first shouts and cries were heard.

The dead king had been found.

PART 1

Chapter 1/Alys

Beaugency, 8 December 1119

It was indecent, that was all there was to it. Indecent.

Now, Hilary, he rebuked himself, *you ought not to be thinking of yourself and the way you are being treated. You should be thinking about Alys.*

He called her face to mind: thin, inquisitive, intelligent, with pale blue eyes and slender, expressive lips. But the memory was already fuzzy at the edges, not quite realised in his mind's eye. Blurring. How was it possible to forget so quickly?

Poor Alys. Dead only one day, and already he couldn't quite recall the exact colour of her hair. He had seen her coffin committed to the ground that very afternoon, the gravediggers shivering as they waited for the burial rites to be completed, leaning on their shovels against the frozen, rutted ground, and eager to resume work filling in the hole they had made, so that they could get warm with the effort. Poor Alys. So sweet natured, so clever, so unreachable. And now – so utterly gone. No amount of poetry could draw her back.

He had loved her… or at least, he had certainly tried his best to. He had strained to develop a powerful passion for his pupil, to make the long days in the castle at Beaugency more lively, and to make sure she made the case for his continued employment. And, of course, wandering scholars did have a certain reputation that had to be upheld: Hilary knew his own weaknesses. He had even penned a series of secret poems dedicated to her, in which he had written: 'Can Sapientia blossom unless the sap of Venus flow?' He envisaged what would happen when she read them, that cool young lady with her pale face and lofty bearing. She would look on him differently, those chilly eyes would soften and, rather than a dishevelled, slightly portly tutor, his monkish tonsure framing a round field of stubble, she would see a romantic hero and they would fall in love, and then...

What awaited them beyond the dangerous revelation of his love for her, he had never really considered. He was sure he would begin to love her if she would only unbend a little and smile once or twice, and perhaps talk of something other than the classics, which seemed to be all that interested her. As her father said, with her nose in the masters of Latin and Greek prose, she was certainly a modern girl.

But before she could read his poems and understand his feelings, Alys had sickened. She became ill at around nones on St Clement's Day, and within hours she was raving that she was being bitten. A physician from the nearby monastery had attended and, after hearing her delirious shrieks of her skin crawling with a thousand ants and witnessing her spasms, announced that she was suffering from St Anthony's Fire. She died a few days later without recognising anyone – paler than ever but scarred with livid blisters – in the depths of Saturday night. Hilary, merely her tutor, had not been allowed to see her once she had become ill and separated from the rest of the household. He had endured the stories from the maids who waited on the sickroom about her sores and her drenching sweats in the frozen nights; he'd seen the ghastly wads of pus-encrusted linen taken from her bedchamber and carried away to be burnt. He had been powerless to help but, then, so had everyone else. There was no cure for the Fire.

She was buried quickly to contain the sickness, even though the ground was so hard it had taken the diggers a full day and night to make enough of a grave to put her in. And after the funeral, as they began to make their way back towards the Great Hall, Alys's father, the Lord of Beaugency, had turned to him and said: 'We shall be sorry to say goodbye to you, Hilary, but you may have an escort as far as the river, if that is any help to you. The cart will be ready whenever you wish to get on your way.'

Hilary had blinked, gaped at him, tucking his icy cold fingers into his sleeves but unable to stop a great chill creeping over his chest. 'My lord?'

'You are a wandering scholar, Hilary. Isn't that what they call you?' said Alys' father. 'Your work here is done. You can hardly stay on without a pupil. It is time for you to go off and ... wander again.'

The afternoon was already beginning to fade. The rushes were burning with an acrid smell, and the outline of the Great Hall of Beaugency, his home for the past two years, was beginning to darken to a silhouette in the winter light. Late afternoon seemed to be merging imperceptibly with dusk, as if the day had never quite carried enough conviction. There were bent figures moving in the distance, pall-bearers back from the chapel, and the distant sound of ladies weeping as they returned to the castle, still shocked at the extinction of Alys. The Lord gives and takes away. Sometimes he just seems to take away.

It was only when his position seemed to slip out of reach that Hilary knew for certain that he hadn't really loved Alys. He had loved his life at the castle, with its food, lamps, firelight and clean straw. He had loved his tiny cell with its iron sconce and writing desk, where he was able to lose himself in poetry, all the while knowing that the aroma drifting up from the kitchens meant that dinner was a certainty. He had loved his pints of ale, and the evenings where stories were told by the fire in the Great Hall, when he might be asked to stand up and entertain them all with a poem or a song. He would pretend reluctance and then perform, declaiming a courtly romance or a comical verse tale, his audience leaning back on stools and trestles and benches.

'Where will I go?' he had said piteously.

'You'll find another pupil,' Alys's father answered. 'A scholar of Ste Genevieve should have no difficulty at all in securing a place. You are well regarded, are you not?'

'Yes,' Hilary replied miserably. That was what he had told him at the beginning, when he had first arrived at the castle. He had been delighted to be believed. It was rare enough for the great lords to employ tutors in their households, and to employ tutors for their daughters was almost unheard of. It was a lazy, fed and magnificent existence and he had very much enjoyed teaching Alys too, despite her preference for books.

'There you are. Now, you will need to be gone before supper, Hilary. I've promised your cell to the clerk.'

*

That was the indecency of it. Alys was barely cold and here he was, out on his ear. The funeral bell was still tolling as he dragged his box of books and belongings across the cobbles of the courtyard, out to the waiting cart.

The servant who was to drive him to the river lifted up the box and flung it on.

'Careful!' shouted Hilary. 'There's a lifetime of copying in that chest.'

The servant, a man he had always disliked, said nothing but gave him a malevolent glance and climbed up into the driving seat. Hilary took his place behind him and wrapped himself as deeply into his woollen cloak as he could. It was freezing and almost dark. Why on earth couldn't they have left tomorrow when it was light?

He imagined his cosy cell now with that distressingly self-satisfied clerk settling down in it, no doubt delighted to have won it from Hilary. He tried to think of where he might be spending the night but could see nothing in his mind's eye but a vast blankness. All he was sure of was that it would be cold and unpleasant.

There are moments in any life when there is no going back, and when the future is still completely shrouded from view. That is where I am, said Hilary to himself. He tried to nurture that forlorn hope that something better awaited him, but it refused to spark into life.

That's the problem with wandering, he thought. You never quite belong anywhere. And if there's no pupil to teach, then it means squires or minor princelings to entertain in return for board, lodging, and maybe a generous change of clothes, and then back on the rutted tracks for the nearest monastery or cathedral. Oh yes, there are worse places to be than in castles and manors, but where will it all lead? Will the day come when I'll find nowhere to lay my head? *Foxes have holes*, *birds of the air have nests* – no, he must not compare himself to Our Lord. This was no time for blasphemy.

Neither of the gate keepers acknowledged him as the cart swayed through the stone portal, clattering a little on the stones. There was hardly anyone to be seen now, and no one seemed to care much that he was leaving. It was true that the household had never really taken to him. Some had disapproved of his poetry, or shared the irritation that servants reserve for those household dependents who consider themselves above menial work. Neither one thing nor the other, that was the fate of tutors everywhere. Hilary liked people to like him and he had fondly imagined that he would win everyone over with his songs and poems, his late night turns in front of the fire. Evidently not. Or perhaps it was worse than that. He was an Englishman, after all, and although he had trained in Paris and was as fluent a French speaker as any native, there was still a trace of his Hampshire accent, and something about him that set him apart. He hadn't spread the fact widely, but Alys had known of it and her father, when in his cups, had jokingly insulted Hilary for his Englishness (or perhaps not so jokingly), so no doubt they all knew it. The fact of being English was not such a crime in itself. It was being different that was the thing.

Still. He tried to put his dejection to one side and think of his future plans, but the bells that had tolled all day still echoed in his head. At least five miles lay between him and the river, an hour's journey in the company of this taciturn servant and the back of a disapproving head, bent slightly over the reins of the horse. He could barely think of anything, as if a huge bruise had covered his available thoughts, too painful to touch, but he pulled himself together and began to ponder his prospects. He had enough money for a few days. He would take a boat into Orléans and offer his services at the college again. There was often work for wandering scholars, especially scholars from the great colleges of Paris, in these rival and provincial seats of learning – though 'provincial' was a word he agreed with himself not to use in the city that considered itself the royal throne of kings.

Orléans was stricter about theology, or so it was said – none of your logic was allowed here – but he could deal with that. If they had no space for him as an assistant, he might have to beg some meals from the monks and then seek out some new master. If that wasn't possible, he might even have to go home to Hampshire to be a hedge-priest or a hayward, or something equally hopeless. But it wasn't as if this was a new predicament. He had been lucky at Beaugency, he knew that, and he might yet be lucky again.

*

It was vespers before they began to approach a small village, with a magnificent castle in the distance and a large inn by the bank of the river. The cart came to a halt.

'Beaugency-sur-Loire,' said his moody guide. 'That's it.'

Mist was rising off the river and obscuring the woods. Nobody was about. The travelling season had been over for more than a month.

'Can't you at least take me to the wharf?' Hilary asked. 'My box is no featherweight.'

Ignoring him, the servant manhandled his chest off the back of the cart. The tension had been in the air since they left the castle. For a moment, Hilary wondered if he was in for some kind of beating. If he was, he calculated he would come off by far the worst in the encounter. It was moments like this when he might just have his throat slit and his body tossed into the Loire. It took another effort of will to rise to his feet and summon up some effort of command.

'All right. Just leave it there. You can go now.'

The servant stared for a moment and seemed to be making up his mind. Then he climbed onto the cart. 'No more boats tonight,' he said, grasping the reins. Then he clicked to urge the horses on and the cart began to pull away. With a sinking sense of abandonment, Hilary watched the cart lurch through the potholes in the gathering gloom. Despite what he had felt about the servant, he would have happily joined him on the journey back to Beaugency and the security of his little cell.

But that life was over now, snuffed out with Alys's existence. He imagined her slender body in its rough coffin, now buried under mounds of icy earth, and sent up a prayer for her soul as he set to work and dragged his box the few hundred yards to the riverside. There was a barge there but, sure enough, the crew were hauling down the sails, and had the definite air of going home about them. Apart from them, there seemed to be nobody around. The only signs of life came from the inn, where lamplight flickered in that peculiarly welcoming hue of gold through the low windows. He thought of a trencher of something hot, a tankard of something comforting, and a warm corner where he could sleep. He had barely enough money to pay for such luxuries and hardly enough energy to speak, let alone to perform in return for them. But he had to find some kind of shelter. He hauled his box towards the inn door.

The door was unlatched and he pushed it open to reveal a murky interior clouded with smoke from the fire. A few other travellers sat about on the great benches, or at the trestles, supping on something that set his mouth watering with its thick, meaty smell. Hilary realised he was famished. When cheap inn slop looked appetising, it was a good sign that a meal was overdue.

A woman approached, sour-faced and carrying a large pitcher of ale.

'Good evening. I am a scholar of Ste-Genevieve,' he said hopefully. 'Might I crave your hospitality this one night?' He drew aside his cloak, and lowered his head to reveal what remained of his tonsure and his semi-monastic status. Surely this was as God-fearing a place as Rouen or Reims, where he had often cadged a bed on the basis of his holy orders.

'Nope,' said the woman. 'We'll have no holy scholars here. No wandering poets neither. No doubt you're about to tell me you'll sing or recite for your supper. Well, we don't want anything of that kind here, thank you.' She stood in front of him, put the pitcher of ale on the table, and then her hands on her ample hips. 'You should see what happened to the last one who sang. Out you go. Go on.'

Hilary felt too tired to argue. It was going to be one of those nights when he slept in his monastic cape under the stars. He began to calculate his chances outside on a freezing night, wondering if he could double back and sneak into the stable. He was too tired even to be angry, wondering where he had hidden his few coins in his luggage.

'You heard me! Shift your arse!' snapped the woman.

A voice came from somewhere in the gloom. 'Leave him be. I'll pay for his supper.'

Hilary looked down the bench, trying to make out who had spoken through the smoke from the tallow candles and lamps. The wind was whispering through the window and making the lamps dance in their pots. Then he saw a pair of bright eyes staring at him in the gloom. The speaker was a man, well wrapped in a travelling cloak, with a dark greying beard and a weathered face. Hilary was too relieved at the unexpected offer even to wonder what had prompted this act of charity. Praise be. I shall eat at least, he thought, gratefully.

The woman shrugged. 'As you wish. But I'll take the money now, if you don't mind.'

As the traveller unwrapped his cloak to reach his purse, Hilary said: 'Who are you, sir? My thanks are due to you. I am in your debt.'

'Say nothing of it,' said the man. His voice was rough and yet had a sing-song lilt, the trace of some accent Hilary could not identify. 'We are riding the same cart, you and I.'

Hilary blinked. 'You're a scholar, too?'

The stranger laughed. 'Do I look like a scholar?'

Hilary peered harder. He said nothing but thought to himself that true scholars tended to look more bedraggled than this man, and less energetic. Nor did they usually carry expensive blades like the one that Hilary could see hanging from his belt.

The landlady stretched her hand out towards the traveller and beckoned rudely for the money. He reached into the red leather pouch that hung around his neck, extracted two coins and pressed them into the rough palm. The landlady looked at them suspiciously for a moment, eyed the two men and then was gone, muttering that she would return presently.

'Come, my friend, eat with me. You look like a cornered stag. We have that in common. I *feel* like a cornered stag. Keep me company tonight and tomorrow we will voyage into Orléans. I'll wager that's where you are going?'

'Yes, that's right…'

'Good. Then sit!' The stranger laughed and Hilary trusted him a little more. He sat down on the bench which was empty apart from his new friend. His eyes had adjusted now, and he could see that the stranger was dressed beneath his cloak in a short tunic over leggings bound with criss-crossed bandages above a pair of stout, short leather boots. He looked as though he had been on the move for many days and was still far from wherever he was going. He gave Hilary a keen glance and said: 'Now, my good clerk-in-holy-orders. Why are you here exactly and with such a forlorn look about you? I know you wandering scholars. Now, let me guess. Gluttony? You stole the wine? I believe the Swedes, a barbaric northern race, think themselves blessed if they drink themselves to death at the holy mass. Come, let us have no secrets between us. We will be companions on the road.'

Hilary stared at him for a moment, taking in everything about the other man. Despite his ease of manner, he seemed to be alert, like a hare in the middle of a field. There was something taut about him, as if he was aware of every noise inside the inn and outside it.

What's he afraid of? Hilary wondered, suspicion prickling on his skin. But, glad of the meal to come at his benefactor's expense, he decided to be friendly and said in a jovial tone: 'I am not quite the wandering scholar you take me for. I am in search of a new place, by God's will. I am a teacher. They call me Hilary the Englishman. As you guessed, I'm on my way to Orléans.'

'Aha. Are you perhaps Hilary the Englishman the poet?'

Hilary blinked at him, astonished. 'You know my poems?'

'I heard them sung at Rouen. I liked them very much and asked who had written something so fine.'

A glow of pleasure spread down Hilary's back and he smiled for the first time that day. He wasn't used to being recognised, and – however exhausting the night, however distant the hope of employment – it cheered his soul. 'I am glad of it, truly. Perhaps you would do me the honour of telling me your own name?'

The stranger laughed again. He nonchalantly flicked something off his tunic. 'Ah, well, that depends who you talk to.'

'Oh yes? And me? What if you're talking to me?'

'To my friends I am usually known as John.'

'John?' Hilary blinked. So that was the accent he had half identified. 'You're English? John of where?'

John looked immediately serious. 'At this moment, I am English, yes. If another were to join us, I might be someone else and from somewhere else. It all depends.'

'What do you mean by that?'

'Come, my friend, how long since you were a plain and simple Englishman, no matter what they called you? You've lived here in France for long enough to know that you can be whatever it suits you to be, whatever it's expedient to be. Isn't that right? You and I are lucky, perhaps, that we can take on the colours that serve us best when necessary.' John smiled and Hilary had the distinct impression that he was supposed to understand what the man was talking about. 'Now, here is our supper. Thanks be to heaven.'

The landlady put down two wooden bowls of stew that seemed to contain hunks of pork and slices of turnip in a murky liquid strongly favoured with dried sage. Dry bread was provided to soak the stew up and Hilary fell on it, ravenous after the long, freezing day, shovelling it in and revelling as the savoury warmth hit his stomach and eased the empty feeling in his blood.

'At least you'll make quick work of it,' the landlady remarked, watching him. 'It isn't godly to burn tallow into the night.' She left them to their meal.

John ate too, a little less frantically but with relish, and then called for ale and cheese, which the landlady brought over with her usual grumpiness. When the platters were cleared, Hilary sat back against the wall, satisfied.

'I needed that,' he said sincerely. 'Thank you, friend.'

'You'd have done the same for me, no doubt, if our situations were reversed. Now, we have an hour or so before I can sleep, if we can persuade the good lady to light another tallow. What do you say to a little gaming?'

'Gaming is a wicked pursuit,' Hilary said piously.

'Come on, indulge me. You may have taken holy orders but you look like a man who has lived to me. I'd bet my cloak you've had your fair share of the gaming table in your time.'

Hillary shrugged. This fellow was perceptive, he'd give him that. It was true that he enjoyed a game or two. Only occasionally, of course. He said lightly: 'Well... perhaps. ...What's your fancy?'

'You can choose. Chess? Tables? Nine-men's morris?'

'You *are* English,' said Hilary. 'Nobody here calls it that.'

John ignored him. 'Excellent, tables it is!'

Hilary wrinkled his nose. He had developed an aversion to tables during his student days in Paris when, for a while, it seemed to be all he did. And it had cost him dear, too.

John reached into the red leather purse at his neck, and Hilary noticed that he had two other large pouches hanging from strings around his neck. Then he banged down a handful of coins on the table. 'I can't stake money,' Hilary said at once. 'I don't have any. Well, hardly any.'

'Never mind. Here. I'll advance you some. And if we can't play for money, we'll play for something else.'

Before Hilary could protest, John had pushed some coins towards him, produced a pair of dice, and the game had begun. Although Hilary hadn't played for a long time, the rules quickly returned to him, for all the good it did him. Within a few throws, he had lost all the coins John had lent him.

'Bad luck, my good clerk-in-holy-orders,' John laughed. 'I'll give you another chance. Here's some more metal.'

The game was on almost at once, and this time Hilary seemed to have a little more luck. He won a few throws and John called for more ale, and they played again. But his fortunes turned once more, and he swiftly lost all the money to his benefactor.

'Ah, you're Fortune's fool tonight, my good Hilary.'

'I think your dice are badly made,' Hilary returned sulkily. He could feel the pull of the game exerting its hold on him. He was hungry to play more, even though he knew the futility of it.

'I've another set of dice here, would you perhaps prefer these?'

'No, no more dice!' said Hilary, a little louder than he had intended. He felt unsure of his words and volume. The ale had certainly taken hold.

John leaned towards him, his flinty eyes shining in the firelight. 'Come on, I can see you want to continue. We don't have to play for money, my friend. How about we play for promises?'

'Promises?'

John nodded. 'Here's my promise to you. If you win the next game, I'll fund your journey to Orleans with a little over for you to enjoy when you get there. But if I win…'

'Yes?' Hilary said suspiciously. He had the sense of having fallen into a trap whose true nature he was yet to discover.

John lifted one of the pouches at his neck. It was large and bulky, made of animal skin, deer by the look of it. 'I've been charged to deliver this to Count Fulk of Anjou, but I've other business I must attend to first and frankly I've managed to get myself into a difficult situation. I can't be in two places at once. If I win, you undertake to deliver the contents of this pouch to Count Fulk, thus freeing me of my obligation.'

'Who? What? All the way to Anjou?' Hilary was indignant.

John smiled. 'It's not so far.' He shrugged. 'Besides, I hear that Count Fulk is looking for a tutor for his sons. You might find that God's hand is in this, guiding you towards Anjou for his purpose.'

'*Your* purpose, more like,' grumbled Hilary, but he could see something in what John said. Perhaps a spell in the delightful environs of Anjou might be rather welcome, especially if there were the prospect of a job. He rather fancied a Christmas in the count's castle; no doubt the wine flowed more freely there than in the monastery of Orleans, where there would be more praying than playing. So, he reflected, if I win I get a journey to Orleans, and if I lose I take the road to Anjou instead. A thought occurred to him and he said craftily: 'If I'm freeing you of your obligation, then it's only right you fund my journey to Anjou, if I end up losing.'

John threw back his head and guffawed. 'You like to try your luck, don't you, friend Hilary? Very well – I agree. You will have money to feed you all the way to Anjou – if you lose, of course. After all, you may win.' John fixed him with an amused look.

'Yes, I may win,' Hilary said, but secretly he was thinking that he had cleverly engineered things so that it was win-win either way as far as he was concerned. He would get a game of tables, and money, win or lose. And if he lost but happened to get a better offer on the way to Anjou and accidentally mislaid the pouch over a hedge, then who would ever know or care? He was unlikely to meet John again, after all.

'Good,' John clashed his tankard against Hilary's and both men drained their ale. 'Here's to the lure of the dice, Hilary!' He held the pair of black pocked cubes out on his palm. 'Shall we play?'

'Play!' declared Hilary, and he watched as they flew from John's hand towards the table, carrying his fate on their spinning faces.

Printed in Great Britain
by Amazon

55786810R00078